92
DICKENS

DATE DUE			

GAYLORD M2

THE IMPORTANCE OF

Charles Dickens

These and other titles are included in The Importance Of biography series:

Alexander the Great	Adolf Hitler
Muhammad Ali	Harry Houdini
Louis Armstrong	Thomas Jefferson
James Baldwin	Mother Jones
Clara Barton	Chief Joseph
The Beatles	Joe Louis
Napoleon Bonaparte	Malcolm X
Julius Caesar	Thurgood Marshall
Rachel Carson	Margaret Mead
Charlie Chaplin	Golda Meir
Charlemagne	Michelangelo
Cesar Chavez	Wolfgang Amadeus Mozart
Winston Churchill	John Muir
Cleopatra	Sir Isaac Newton
Christopher Columbus	Richard M. Nixon
Hernando Cortes	Georgia O'Keeffe
Marie Curie	Louis Pasteur
Charles Dickens	Pablo Picasso
Emily Dickinson	Elvis Presley
Amelia Earhart	Jackie Robinson
Thomas Edison	Norman Rockwell
Albert Einstein	Eleanor Roosevelt
Duke Ellington	Anwar Sadat
Dian Fossey	Margaret Sanger
Benjamin Franklin	Oskar Schindler
Galileo Galilei	John Steinbeck
Emma Goldman	Tecumseh
Jane Goodall	Jim Thorpe
Martha Graham	Mark Twain
Lorraine Hansberry	Queen Victoria
Stephen Hawking	Pancho Villa
Jim Henson	H. G. Wells

THE IMPORTANCE OF

Charles Dickens

by Eleanor H. Ayer

Lucent Books, P.O. Box 289011, San Diego, CA 92198-9011

Library of Congress Cataloging-in-Publication Data

Ayer, Eleanor H.
   The importance of Charles Dickens / by Eleanor H. Ayer.
      p.   cm.—(The importance of)
   Includes bibliographical references and index.
   Summary: Discusses the life and works of the prolific
nineteenth-century British writer, known for such works as
"Oliver Twist," "A Christmas Carol," "American Notes," and
"A Tale of Two Cities."
   ISBN 1-56006-525-7 (lib. bdg. : alk. paper)
   1. Dickens, Charles, 1812–1870—Biography—Juvenile
literature.   2. Novelists, English—19th century—Biography—
Juvenile literature.   [1. Dickens, Charles, 1812–1870.
2. Authors, English.]   I. Title.   II. Series.
  PR4581.A94   1998
  823'.8—dc21   97-34957
  [B]   CIP
                                                    AC

Copyright 1998 by Lucent Books, Inc., P.O. Box 289011,
San Diego, California 92198-9011

Printed in the U.S.A.

Contents

Foreword

THE IMPORTANCE OF biography series deals with individuals who have made a unique contribution to history. The editors of the series have deliberately chosen to cast a wide net and include people from all fields of endeavor. Individuals from politics, music, art, literature, philosophy, science, sports, and religion are all represented. In addition, the editors did not restrict the series to individuals whose accomplishments have helped change the course of history. Of necessity, this criterion would have eliminated many whose contribution was great, though limited. Charles Darwin, for example, was responsible for radically altering the scientific view of the natural history of the world. His achievements continue to impact the study of science today. Others, such as Chief Joseph of the Nez Percé, played a pivotal role in the history of their own people. While Joseph's influence does not extend much beyond the Nez Percé, his nonviolent resistance to white expansion and his continuing role in protecting his tribe and his homeland remain an inspiration to all.

These biographies are more than factual chronicles. Each volume attempts to emphasize an individual's contributions both in his or her own time and for posterity. For example, the voyages of Christopher Columbus opened the way to European colonization of the New World. Unquestionably, his encounter with the New World brought monumental changes to both Europe and the Americas in his day. Today, however, the broader impact of Columbus's voyages is being critically scrutinized. *Christopher Columbus,* as well as every biography in The Importance Of series, includes and evaluates the most recent scholarship available on each subject.

Each author includes a wide variety of primary and secondary source quotations to document and substantiate his or her work. All quotes are footnoted to show readers exactly how and where biographers derive their information, as well as provide stepping stones to further research. These quotations enliven the text by giving readers eyewitness views of the life and times of each individual covered in The Importance Of series.

Finally, each volume is enhanced by photographs, bibliographies, chronologies, and comprehensive indexes. For both the casual reader and the student engaged in research, The Importance Of biographies will be a fascinating adventure into the lives of people who have helped shape humanity's past and present, and who will continue to shape its future.

IMPORTANT DATES IN THE LIFE OF CHARLES DICKENS

1812
Charles John Huffam Dickens born in Portsmouth, England, on February 7
1817
Moves to Chatham
1822
Moves to London
1827
Formal education ends; begins work for two legal firms
1833
First creative story published, "A Dinner at Poplar Walk"
1834
Begins using the pen name "Boz"
1835
Contributes stories to the *Evening Chronicle*; engagement to Catherine Hogarth
1836
Sketches by Boz published February 7; first issue of *The Pickwick Papers* appears April 1; marries Catherine Hogarth
1837
First installment of *Oliver Twist* published
1838
First installment of *Nicholas Nickleby* published
1840
The Old Curiosity Shop begins serialization in Dickens's new magazine, *Master Humphrey's Clock*
1841
Barnaby Rudge published
1842
Tours America and publishes *American Notes*
1843
Martin Chuzzlewit begins serialization; *A Christmas Carol* published
1844
Lives with family in Italy

1846
Begins the *Daily News; Pictures from Italy* published; family lives in Switzerland and Paris; first installments of *Dombey and Son*
1849
First installment of *David Copperfield*
1850
First issue of *Household Words*
1851
A Child's History of England begins serialization; first installment of *Bleak House*
1854
Hard Times begins serialization
1855
First installment of *Little Dorrit*
1856
Writes the play *The Frozen Deep*
1858
Charles and Catherine separate; increased schedule of public readings
1859
First issue of *All the Year Round*; serialization of *A Tale of Two Cities*
1860
First installment of *Great Expectations*
1864
Our Mutual Friend begins serialization
1867
Embarks on reading tour of United States
1868
Begins reading tour of Britain
1869
Begins writing *The Mystery of Edwin Drood*
1870
Dickens dies June 9

The Greatest English Novelist

Called the greatest English novelist by many literary experts, Charles Dickens was more popular in his lifetime than any previous author. "Charles Dickens belongs to all the world," writes professor Edgar Johnson. "He is a titan of literature . . . himself a Dickens character."[1] In millions of minds, "Dickens is still billed as Britain's 'best-loved' writer of fiction."[2] Novelist and professor Vladimir Nabokov once confessed to his students, "If it were possible I would like to devote the fifty minutes of every class meeting to mute meditation, concentration, and admiration, of Dickens."[3]

On a list of the best-known English authors of all time, Charles Dickens ranks at the top with William Shakespeare. He was read by (or to) some of the poorest, least educated people of Britain, as well as by Queen Victoria and her court. When he died in 1870, he was mourned by readers around the world.

Unlike many authors, musicians, or artists whose genius is appreciated only after their death, Charles Dickens gained fame while he was young and remained popular throughout his lifetime. His books have been read extensively by every generation worldwide since the mid-1830s.

Dickens's fame did not come easily. Too often, Dickens once noted to a friend, people assume that writing is "the easiest amuse-ment in the world." They don't realize that to be a good writer one needs "such elements as patience, study, punctuality, determination, self-denial, training of mind and body, hours of application and seclusion."[4]

To be as productive a writer as Charles Dickens also required tremendous self-discipline in keeping a daily schedule. During his lifetime he wrote sixteen major novels, hundreds of short stories and essays, plays, and articles, and served as the founder or editor of several magazines and newspapers. He turned his natural restlessness and energy into an extensive body of writing, becoming one of the most varied and imaginative authors of all time.

Forever a Popular Figure

Whatever the author's mood—comical, tender, melancholy, aggrieved, pessimistic, or hopeful—Dickens's public adored him. The feeling was mutual. Biographer Peter Ackroyd writes that Dickens was "always concerned with his audience and with the effect he was having upon that audience." He wanted his writing to have "direct and immediate appeal."[5] When his books were read aloud, he wanted them to make an equal impact on listeners. The author's public appearances had an especially

"Please, Sir, I Want Some More"

One of Dickens's major themes was the plight of the poor. With stunning impact, he showed how the weak and disadvantaged are victimized. In Oliver Twist, *orphan Oliver grows up in a workhouse, with little to wear and less to eat. One night he speaks out daringly at supper, uttering a request that he knows could bring him death.*

"The gruel disappeared; the boys whispered to each other, and winked at Oliver; while his next neighbours nudged him. Child as he was, he was desperate with hunger, and reckless with misery. He rose from the table; and advancing to the master, basin and spoon in hand, said: somewhat alarmed at his own temerity:

'Please, sir, I want some more.'

The master was a fat, healthy man; but he turned very pale. He gazed in stupefied astonishment on the small rebel for some seconds, and then clung for support to the copper [kettle].

The assistants were paralysed with wonder; the boys with fear.

'What!' said the master at length, in a faint voice.

'Please, sir,' replied Oliver, 'I want some more.'

The master aimed a blow at Oliver's head with the ladle; pinioned him in his arms; and shrieked aloud for [help]."

Oliver asks for more gruel as his fellow orphans listen attentively to the proceedings.

dramatic flair. His acting talents made him an excellent public speaker and he was said to be the best after-dinner entertainer of his time.

His vibrant personality and appearance hinted of the success that was later to come. Looking back to the time of his first novel's release, biographer John Forster writes in *The Life of Charles Dickens*, "[His face] seemed to tell so little of a student or writer of books, and so much of a man of action and business in the world. Light and motion flashed from every part of it."[6]

Dickens wrote during the reign of Queen Victoria (1838–1901), one of the most glorious periods in English history. During this time, the British Empire became the most important power in the world, and London was the center of the British Empire. It was also the center of Charles Dickens's world. "London entered his soul; it terrified him and it entranced him,"[7] writes Peter Ackroyd.

It was an age of good manners and respectable living and a moral code modern society would consider prudish. Charles Dickens was a supremely Victorian figure, but the timeless qualities of his writing transcend the Victorian age, as each generation rediscovers his unique appeal.

Chapter

1 "The Secret Agony of My Soul"

To begin my life with the beginning of my life, I record that I was born (as I have been informed and believe) on a Friday, at twelve o'clock at night. It was remarked that the clock began to strike, and I began to cry, simultaneously.

—Dickens, *David Copperfield*

So Dickens recorded the entry into this world of the hero of his novel *David Copperfield*. His own birth was similar, occurring on a Friday, February 7, 1812, not long after midnight. "As an adult," writes professor Fred Kaplan, "he considered Friday his lucky day, needing to believe that he had been born with great expectations and the talent and will to realize them."[8] Charles John Huffam Dickens joined a sister, Frances Elizabeth, called Fanny.

The Dickens Family Tree

The house where Dickens was born, at 387 Mile End Terrace in Portsmouth, was a narrow one in a long row of buildings, a comfortable place that his parents rented. John, his father, was "a loquacious, industrious man with a rather charming theatrical flair,"[9] writes biographer Brian Murray.

For seven years, he had been employed as a clerk in the navy pay office, first in London and then in Portsmouth. His salary should have been enough to support his family but, notes Kaplan, "he was thought careless with money, irresponsible about

The house at 387 Mile End Terrace, where Charles Dickens was born. Like the hero in David Copperfield, *Dickens was born around midnight.*

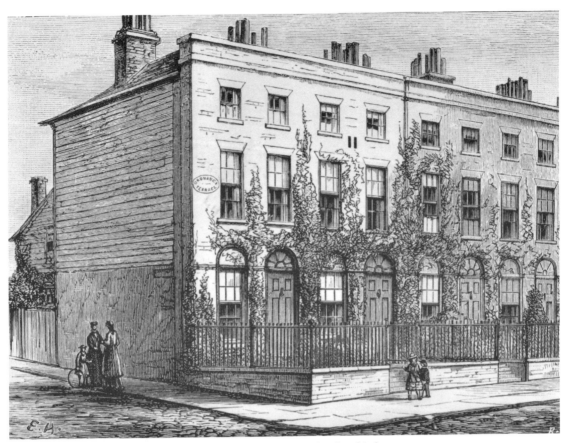

Charles Dickens remembered spending the best years of his boyhood at his home in Chatham (pictured). During these years, the Dickens family experienced a period of financial stability.

work, and too eager to enjoy the pleasures of conviviality [drinking, feasting, socializing]."[10] Just four months after Charles's birth his father, beleaguered by money problems, moved the family to a cheaper, more modest home.

Charles's mother, Elizabeth, was a slim, hazel-eyed woman who enjoyed a good time as much as her husband. Only hours before Charles's birth, she had been attending a ball. His parents treated his arrival with joy, and he was welcomed into what would become a family of eight children, two of whom died in infancy.

The Happy Childhood Years

When Charles was two, his father was transferred to London, and two years later to Chatham, southeast of London. "This period of relative prosperity was the peak of the family fortunes," writes one biographer, "and Charles Dickens always looked back upon it as the golden age of his childhood."[11] In Chatham, he spent the best years of his youth.

The golden age lasted from 1817 to 1822, and although his father's financial troubles were brewing, Charles was blissfully unaware. Chatham, said his good friend John Forster, was the birthplace of Dickens's creativity. The house in Chatham had "a cheerful rhythm":

> The boy next door . . . had a magic lantern which fascinated Charles; Lucy Stroughill, a pretty girl on whom Charles doted, seemed to lead a life of birthdays and to be brought up entirely on cake, wine, and presents. There were . . . parties for all the occasions—Christmas and Twelfth Night and Guy Fawkes Day—and outings to the circus and the pantomime.[12]

In Chatham, Charles and his siblings were cared for by nursemaid Mary Weller. Mary had a taste for the macabre and told the children great tales of ghosts and ghouls, deaths and birthings. She loved to scare them and would often begin an evening's tales with moans and groans or terrifying shrieks. One of her favorite characters, Captain Murderer, killed his various wives, baked them in meat pies, and ate them.

His mother taught Charles to read. Among his favorite books were *Robinson Crusoe, Don Quixote, Tom Jones,* and especially the *Arabian Nights.* Charles's passion for reading was due partly to the fact that he was a sickly child and was never very good at sports or games. He was, according to John Forster, "subject to attacks of violent spasm [seizures] which disabled him for any active exertion."[13] Instead, Charles spent hours organizing plays with involved plots, props, music, and dancing.

He and Fanny attended a school located above a dyer's shop, where the teacher's spiteful dog attacked students going up the stairs. The teacher was a strict and severe old woman who struck fear in the hearts of her pupils. After two years and another family move, the children went to the Classical, Mathematical, and Commercial School; there Charles very much enjoyed an in-depth education in the arts and sciences. Although he always hoped for a longer, more complete education, he got little beyond the years at Chatham.

A House of Death and Debt

When Charles turned ten, his happy childhood ended. His father was transferred back to London, where he sank deeper and deeper into debt. The family, now numbering eight, moved to a smaller, cheaper, four-room house, but even that did not help stave off a financial crisis. In the months that followed, they were forced to pawn many possessions. Hard times turned to grief with the death of Harriet, Charles's three-year-old sister.

In desperation, Elizabeth opened a school, known as Mrs. Dickens's Establishment. But the enterprise, which was ill conceived and poorly planned, ended in failure. She had no experience as a teacher, no money, and knew no families who could afford to send their children to her school. The money that should have paid family bills went instead to renting a larger house that could accommodate the school. But no one attended—not one student. Yet neither John nor Elizabeth seemed to grasp the magnitude of their situation.

On February 20, 1824, John Dickens was arrested for debt and taken to jail. Three days later he was moved to the Marshalsea, a debtors' prison, the horrid hellhole that Dickens writes about in *Little*

Dorrit. In chapter 6, he describes the place in vivid detail:

> It had stood there many years before, and it remained there some years afterwards; but it is gone now, and the world is none the worse without it. . . . It was an oblong pile of barrack buildings, partitioned in squalid houses standing back to back, so that there were no back rooms; environed by a narrow paved yard, hemmed in by high walls duly spiked at top.[14]

A government report at the time of John's imprisonment showed that "the prison yard overflowed with waste water and that the open drains were 'sometimes choked and offensive' and smelled bad." Never-

Unable to pay his overwhelming debt, John Dickens (pictured), Charles's father, was confined to a debtors' prison. Dickens later wrote about the prison in Little Dorrit.

theless, the report declared the place "tolerably clean."[15]

His father's imprisonment led to further hardships for Charles. Although his sister Fanny, a talented musician, had been attending the Royal Academy of Music on scholarship and so was allowed to continue despite her father's situation, Charles had to quit school and go to work. His mother and siblings moved with John into bleak, barren rooms at the Marshalsea, which was not uncommon for debtors' families. Charles, now twelve years old, boarded at a home across town and worked a series of odd jobs.

On Sundays he and Fanny went to the Marshalsea to visit the family. There he witnessed firsthand the life of the other inmates and pressed his mother to tell him all that went on. John fancied himself superior to the other prisoners, an unfortunate member of the cultural elite for whom poverty was the result of temporary bad luck. William Dorrit, the imprisoned father in *Little Dorrit*, adopted a similar attitude, proclaiming himself "Father of the Marshalsea" because of his longtime residence.

A Sentence in Hell

In hopes of helping the Dickenses, friend James Lamert offered Charles a job at Warren's Blacking Factory, where he was a manager. Charles's father considered the offer a stroke of good fortune, but for his son it was a sentence in hell. Warren's was located in a warehouse along London's Strand which Dickens described as a "crazy, tumble-down old house . . . literally overrun with rats."[16] The company made a black paste that was applied to boots and fire grates to protect

"Being Utterly Without Hope"

The grim reality of life at Warren's Blacking Factory temporarily dashed Charles's hopes and dreams. He wrote of the experience twice, once in a letter to John Forster, and again in nearly identical terms in these lines from the autobiographical David Copperfield.

"No words can express the secret agony of my soul as I sunk into this companionship; compared these henceforth everyday associates with those of my happier childhood . . . and felt my hopes of growing up to be a learned and distinguished man crushed in my bosom. The deep remembrance of the sense I had of being utterly without hope now; of the shame I felt in my position; of the misery it was to my young heart to believe that day by day what I had learned, and thought, and delighted in, and raised my fancy and my emulation up by, would pass away from me, little by little, never to be brought back any more; I mingled my tears with the water in which I was washing the bottles; and sobbed as if there were a flaw in my own breast, and it were in danger of bursting."

Warren's Blacking Factory, where the twelve-year-old Charles worked labeling pots of blacking. The experience profoundly affected his future.

them from wear and weathering. Charles's job was to cover pots of paste-blacking with oil paper and a blue cover sheet, tie them with string, trim the edges, and paste labels on them. Writes Peter Ackroyd: "That warehouse, and his work there covering the tops of paste-blacking, never left his memory. He always recalled the rats, the dirt, the decay, and the old tumbling building lurching over towards the river, the river which was now bearing away the hopes of his childhood."[17]

Charles refused to fit into the role of a bleak factory worker, and he considered himself a cut above the "common men and boys," the "common companions" in the blacking factory. They were born poor and would stay that way; he would not. The other boys, in turn, recognized Charles's potential, referring to him as "the young gentleman."

Altogether, Charles worked nearly a year at the blacking factory, twelve hours every day except Sunday. He spent his free time walking the streets of London, a pastime that became a lifelong habit. Nearly all his books contain detailed descriptions of the city in its raw, undecorated form, such as this one in *Little Dorrit*:

> It was a Sunday evening in London, gloomy, close, and stale. . . . Melancholy streets, in a penitential garb of soot, steeped the souls of the people who were condemned to look at them out of windows, in dire despondency. In every thoroughfare, up almost every alley, and down almost every turning, some doleful bell was throbbing, jerking, tolling, as if the Plague were in the city and the dead-carts were going round.[18]

After John had been in the Marshalsea several months his mother died, leaving him a small inheritance. The poor housekeeper had managed her money far better than her spendthrift son. This good fortune allowed him to arrange a settlement with his creditors and go free.

"I Never Shall Forget"

Charles imagined that his father's release from prison would mean his own release from the blacking factory, but he was nearly wrong. John, humiliated by the grief he had caused his son, visited Warren's upon his release. Appalled by the conditions in which his son was working, he got into a heavy argument with Charles's boss, which ended the boy's employment. Charles was delighted, but his mother, unwilling to lose the additional income, smoothed over the argument and got her son reinstated. Dickens never forgave her. Much later he wrote, "[I] never afterwards forgot, I never shall forget, I never can forget, that my mother was warm for my being sent back."[19]

Elizabeth's decision was overridden, however, by John's firm announcement that the boy would attend the Wellington House Academy, a private school, not return to work. Charles quickly readapted to student life and did well in his studies, although he was critical of the teachers. The headmaster, he later wrote, was "by far the most ignorant man I have ever had the pleasure to know, who was one of the worst-tempered men perhaps that ever lived, whose business it was to take as much out of us and to put as little into us as possible."[20]

Dickens remained at Wellington House for two years. He might have stayed

Dickens's Assessment of Women

Elizabeth Dickens's attempts to keep Charles at the blacking factory colored his view of women. In The World of Charles Dickens *August Wilson explains Dickens's impatience with women.*

"On his mother, he formed early his expectations of what a woman could fail to be. The separation between Dickens's view of life and his mother's . . . caused him to see her (and subsequently so many women) only with irritated impatience. . . . Mrs. Dickens had ambitions for him, but her ambitions were the very limited, practical ones of her class and sex. . . . She set him at the foot of the ladder at Warren's; subsequently . . . by using her 'connections', she helped him to a higher but still very humble rung."

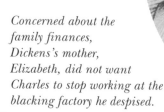

Concerned about the family finances, Dickens's mother, Elizabeth, did not want Charles to stop working at the blacking factory he despised.

longer but for another downturn in his father's finances. In 1827, when he was fifteen, what he called his "irregular rambling education"[21] came to an end.

The events of the past three to four years had made an indelible mark on Dickens. His father's financial failures left him insecure and fearful. London had become what Peter Ackroyd called "a place of imprisonment and suffocation. . . . So it is that in his fiction he returns again and again to the same areas . . . all these places being the sites of his youthful anguish and humiliation."[22]

Although he rarely spoke about his past, his writing makes it clear that the memories of those years were never far below the surface. The image of the lost, oppressed, despairing child is present in many Dickens novels.

Chapter

2 "My Eyes Were So Dimmed with Joy and Pride"

He wore a frock-coat buttoned up, of dark blue cloth, trousers to match, and . . . [a] black neckerchief, but no shirt collar showing. His complexion was of a healthy pink—almost glowing— rather a round face, fine forehead, beautiful expressive eyes full of animation, a firmly-set mouth, a good-sized rather straight nose. . . . His hair was a beautiful brown, and worn long, as was then the fashion. . . . His appearance was altogether decidedly military.

—A colleague's description of Dickens as a young law clerk, from Ackroyd, *Dickens*

The fifteen-year-old Charles Dickens was now a clerk in the legal firm of Ellis and Blackmore. Using her "connections," his mother had gotten the job for Charles when the family's finances required that he quit school. Blackmore, the partner who hired him, thought Charles "exceedingly good looking and clever." Dickens quickly proved him right. "His knowledge of London was wonderful, for he could describe the position of every shop in any of the West End streets." [23]

For a short time, Charles worked at Ellis and Blackmore. This job was decidedly better than the blacking factory, but he was lit- tle more than an errand boy. Impatient to find more interesting work, he quit to take a position with the firm of Charles Molloy but found that job much the same. These jobs did teach him two things, however. One was that he did not want to pursue a legal career. The other was the tremendously useful skill of shorthand. In just a short time, Dickens learned to take shorthand with exceeding speed and accuracy that helped him greatly in his future career.

A period of unemployment followed the clerking jobs, during which he applied for a reader's ticket, which allowed him access to books at the British Museum. Always an avid reader, Charles devoted himself for the next year "to the acquirement of such general literature as I could pick up in the Library of the British Museum." [24]

John Dickens, impressed by his son's mastery of shorthand, learned the skill himself after losing his government job and ultimately entered the field of journalism. At eighteen Charles began a similar career, as a reporter at Doctors' Commons, site of the offices of various legal firms and courts. The shorthand reporters recorded the proceedings of the courts, which Charles found as dull as his previous clerking jobs.

While working at Doctors' Commons, Dickens honed his shorthand skills. He also formed highly critical impressions of

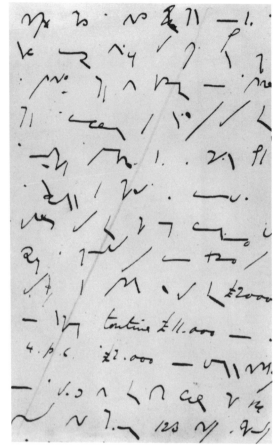

A page of Dickens's shorthand notes. Dickens learned shorthand as a clerk in legal firms, and the skill greatly helped him in finding work.

lawyers—"monkish attorneys," he called them. Here he witnessed firsthand many of the faults of the outdated British legal system, such as the ridiculously long cases dragged on in the courts, which he later criticized in his novels.

First Love

During this time, Dickens experienced his first and perhaps strongest love. The girl was Maria Beadnell, daughter of a London banker, whom he met through a clerk friend at the bank. Charles was welcomed at the Beadnell household, but it was apparent that he was a social inferior, in a class referred to as "shabby-genteel." He had no promising future.

Determined to impress Maria's family, Charles threw himself into acting, a career looked upon askance by conservative businessmen like her father but one for which Dickens had particular talent. Often he practiced "four, five, six hours a day: shut up in my own room, or walking about in the fields. I prescribed to myself, too, a . . . system for learning parts; and learnt a great number."[25]

Although he was successful at getting acting roles, his efforts at romance were fruitless. Concerned about their daughter's involvement with a man Mrs. Beadnell absently called "Mr. Dickin," they sent Maria to Paris to complete her schooling. "My whole being," wrote Dickens, "was blighted by the Angel of my soul"[26] being sent away.

It was bad enough to have her gone. But it was worse when she returned and proved to be a heartless tease, encouraging him one minute and rejecting him the next. After she harshly criticized one of his theatrical performances he wrote her, "Our meetings of late have been little more than so many displays of heartless indifference on the one hand while on the other they have never failed to prove a fertile source of wretchedness."[27]

Eventually Dickens put the affair behind him, but it left him a changed person. Although he married another woman and fathered ten children, his love for his wife was never as great as his early passion for Maria. In *David Copperfield*, he brought to life certain of Maria's qualities in Dora, who had smitten the hero, David. (Wrote biographer Edgar Johnson, "Only in the disguised form of David Copperfield . . . could he make confessional to the world."[28])

All was over in a moment. I had fulfilled my destiny. I was a captive and a slave. I loved Dora Spenlow to distraction!

She was more than human to me. She was a Fairy, a Sylph, I don't know what she was—anything that no one ever saw, and everything that everybody ever wanted. I was swallowed up in an abyss of love in an instant. There was no pausing on the brink; no looking

The Devastating Beadnell Affair

Charles's passion for Maria Beadnell did not die easily. In their book Dickens: A Life, *Norman and Jeanne MacKenzie describe Dickens's last, desperate attempt to win her favor. On May 19, 1833, he wrote to tell her that all past problems and grievances would be forgotten, if only they could begin again:*

"There is nothing I have more at heart, nothing I more sincerely and earnestly desire, than to be reconciled to you. . . . I have never loved and I never can love any human creature breathing but yourself. . . . Absence . . . has not altered my feelings in the slightest degree, and the Love I now tender you is as pure, and as lasting as at any period of our former correspondence."

Henry Austin painted this fanciful portrait of Maria Beadnell for Dickens in 1831.

down, or looking back; I was gone, head-long, before I had sense to say a word to her.[29]

Maria's rejection deeply affected Charles's ability to show love and affection toward other people. He later told his friend Forster that the whole affair developed in him "a habit of suppression [that] I know is no part of my original nature, but which makes me chary [wary] of showing my affections, even to my children, except when they are very young."[30] Some friends speculated that Maria's rejection pushed him into an early marriage that he otherwise might not have pursued.

A Reporter and Actor

During this time, Dickens was admitted to the reporters' gallery at the House of Commons in Parliament, where his father was a reporter. He worked on a freelance basis at first, selling his stories to various publications and sharpening his skills to become the best shorthand reporter in London journalistic circles. His new position filled him with a love for journalism and a hatred for both the law and Parliament.

In 1832, thanks again to his mother's connections, Charles joined the staff of the *Mirror of Parliament*, a paper started by his uncle John Henry Barrow four years earlier. By now the Barrows "had begun to realize that their young nephew had ability as well as ambition."[31] At the *Mirror* he worked as a parliamentary reporter. But to indulge his fanciful mind and his liberal political bent, he became a reporter for a new, radical paper, *True Sun*, which began publication the same year.

Now that he had a little money in his pocket, Dickens began attending plays nearly every night. George Lear, a fellow law clerk, recalled how "he could imitate, in a manner I have never heard equalled, the low population of the streets of London in all their varieties."[32] A friend recalled that Dickens "believed he had more talent for the drama than for literature, [and] he certainly had more delight in acting than in any other work whatever."[33] His friend and biographer John Forster agreed that he could imitate or improvise exquisitely, but thought he fell short in the more traditional sense of acting:

> [He] had the powers of projecting himself into shapes and suggestions of fancy which is one of the marvels of

If not for a cold that kept him from an audition, Dickens might have ended up an actor.

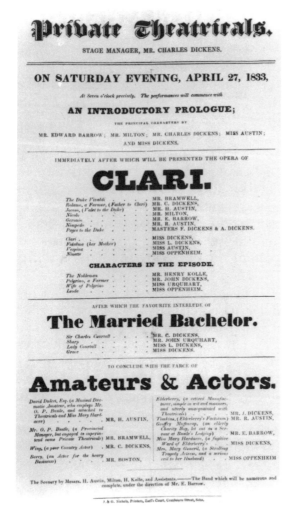

A playbill advertises an amateur theater performance directed by Charles that includes his sister in the cast.

theater manager, "and a natural power of reproducing in my own person what I observed in others."[35] When the day came, however, Dickens had a severe cold that caused his face to swell, and he was forced to cancel the audition. Peter Ackroyd considers the cancellation a stroke of luck:

> Never can there have been a more fortunate illness. He would not have been a great stage actor; he was too small for romantic leads, and there was a certain spareness and lightness about him which would have made him suitable really only for servants, dandies and assorted comic roles. The stage was not his destiny, and so he became ill on the day which that particular future opened for him. Somehow he knew—or at least his body knew—that this was not the life for which he was intended.[36]

Historian and novelist Angus Wilson agrees that fate may have been kind to Charles Dickens the actor. "One can only say that, by even the most friendly accounts, he could gravely misdoubt his own talents in some of the roles he chose to represent in the amateur theatre."[37]

Boz Is Born

A year after the foiled Covent Garden audition, Charles Dickens submitted his first creative story for publication. "He dropped his first manuscript into a letter box," writes biographer Stephen Leacock, "posting it after dark with stealth and fear."[38] The piece, titled "A Dinner at Poplar Walk," was sent to the *Monthly Magazine*. One night in December 1833, he picked up a copy of the magazine just

creative imagination, and what he desired to express he became. . . . [But his talent] was rather in the vividness and variety of his assumptions than in the completeness, finish, or ideality he could give to any part of them.[34]

Near his twentieth birthday he arranged for a stage audition at Covent Garden. "I believed I had a strong perception of character and oddity," he told the

An illustration dramatizes Dickens submitting his first story for publication at the offices of the Monthly Magazine.

off the press. To his delight, his article was there; his mind went wild with visions of literary success. "I walked down to Westminster Hall and turned into it for half an hour, because my eyes were so dimmed with joy and pride that they could not bear the street and were not fit to be seen there."[39]

The publisher asked Dickens for more, and he responded with nine other sketches. His story in the August 1834 issue was signed "Boz," the nickname of his youngest brother, Augustus. "Boz," recalled Dickens, "was a very familiar household word to me, long before I was an author."[40] It would soon be a household

word to the world, but for now Boz's identity was kept a secret.

Also in August 1834, Dickens accepted a parliamentary reporting job with the *Morning Chronicle* newspaper. Unlike the *Mirror of Parliament*, published only when Parliament was in session, the *Chronicle* was a daily paper. When there were no parliamentary sessions to record, Dickens became a political reporter. In addition to reporting, his editor, John Black, encouraged him to submit sketches to the *Chronicle*, which he did beginning in September 1834. Black was, according to the young author, "my first hearty out-and-out appreciator."[41]

On the last day of January 1835, the publisher of the *Morning Chronicle* launched a new paper, the *Evening Chronicle*, published three times weekly and edited by George Hogarth. Beginning with the first issue, Hogarth asked Dickens to contribute stories. He did so willingly, but not without asking if he might have "claim to *some* additional remuneration."[42] Predictably, his father was deep in debt and Charles needed money to help keep him out of debtors' prison. He was granted the raise.

He found his work for the *Chronicle* a sheer joy and later credited his first successes to "the wholesome training of severe newspaper work when I was a very young man." He respected the watchdog role that the press played in society, calling it "the great public safeguard" and "the axis on which the moral world turned."[43] And, of course, the sketches allowed him to indulge his creative talent. This, combined with his journalist's eye for facts, created the core of Dickens's success as a social novelist. His time working on the liberal *Morning Chronicle* had a major effect on his political outlook.

The Influence of the Hogarth Family

Editor George Hogarth was much impressed by Dickens's spirited enthusiasm for reporting and quickly became friends with the younger man, taking him home to meet his family. His eldest child was nineteen-year-old Catherine, called Kate, "a pretty girl with a rosy complexion, heavy-lidded blue eyes, and a slightly retroussé [turned-up] nose."[44] Her sister Mary was also very attractive, but she was only fourteen. Socially the Hogarths were much like the "shabby-genteel" Dickenses, but they did claim some influential acquaintances such as Scottish writer and poet Sir Walter Scott and Scottish poet Robert Burns.

Always the entertainer, Dickens amused Kate, Mary, and their two younger sisters with his acting and mimicry. By early 1835, the attraction between Kate and Charles was mutual. After attending his twenty-third birthday party, she wrote her cousin that she "enjoyed it very much. Mr. Dickens improves . . . on acquaintance, he is very gentlemanly and pleasant."[45]

Unlike the outgoing and outspoken Charles, Kate was rather shy and sulked like a child when she felt slighted. It was clear from the start that Dickens would set the rules in the relationship. He insisted in his letters that "she was not to manipulate

A sketch portrays Charles Dickens, his future wife, Catherine, and her sister Mary. In many ways Dickens got along better with Mary than with his wife.

Sketches by Boz

Dickens's Sketches by Boz, *published February 7, 1836, was an unexpected success. In an essay on door knockers, Dickens demonstrates the superb wit and dry humor that made his sketches so effective.*

"Whenever we visit a man for the first time, we contemplate the features of his knocker with the greatest curiosity, for we well know that, between the man and his knocker, there will inevitably be a greater or less degree of resemblance and sympathy. . . . If ever you find a man changing his habitation without any reasonable pretext, depend upon it that, although he may not be aware of the fact himself, it is because he and his knocker are at variance. This is a new theory, but we venture to launch it, nevertheless, as being quite as ingenious and infallible as many thousand of the learned speculations which are daily broached for public good and private fortune-making."

him with feminine wiles or pettish moods . . . and when he reproved her she was expected to admit her faults and seek to mend her ways."[46]

The affair with Maria Beadnell had left Dickens wary of a close relationship, afraid of being rejected and hurt again. In May 1835, he and Kate became engaged, but a short time later, after she snubbed him slightly, he wrote that her attitude had both surprised and hurt him:

> surprised, because I could not have believed that such sullen and inflexible ob-

stinacy could exist in the breast of any girl in whose heart love had found a place; and hurt . . . because I feel for you more than I have ever professed, and feel a slight from you more than I care to tell. . . . If three weeks or three months of my society has wearied you, do not trifle with me, using me like any other toy as suits your humour for the moment.[47]

Throughout his life, Dickens kept a certain distance in his personal relationships, protecting himself against the possibility of emotional pain.

3 A Sudden and Astounding Rise to Eminence

Pickwick is at length begun in all his might and glory.

—Dickens to his publisher,
February 18, 1836

The success of *Sketches by Boz* attracted the attention of William Hall, the bookseller from whom Dickens had bought the issue of *Monthly Magazine* containing his first published story. Hall and his partner in a publishing business, Edward Chapman, had watched Dickens's success with interest. Now they approached him with a proposal: to write humorous sketches to accompany a series of illustrations by the well-known artist Robert Seymour. These sketches would depict "the adventures of a 'Nimrod Club' of Cockney sportsmen." Dickens was interested, but replied that he "had no personal taste for hunting, shooting, or fishing, and that he thought that line of humour had been overdone." [48]

Neither did he want the text to be secondary to the illustrations. He proposed instead a series of humorous adventures based on the activities of the Pickwick Club, an organization devoted to doing "researches into the quaint and curious phenomena of life." [49] The book, he suggested, should be published in monthly installments, making it more affordable to the poor. Seymour was not enthused by the change in format, but he agreed rather than see the project die.

An Unpromising Start

The first of twenty installments of the *Posthumous Papers of the Pickwick Club* appeared on April 1, 1836. Chapman and Hall began an ambitious advertising campaign to promote the new serial, but sales were flat and the second issue was reduced from a thousand copies to five hundred. Moreover, Seymour was upset. His drawings were often unsatisfactory to Dickens or the publishers, perhaps because he could not get the original plan for the project out of his mind. Nor could he shake off some resentment of Dickens for taking over his idea.

Although not a failure, *Pickwick* was far from a success. "[It] is one of those books so world-famous," writes critic Angus Wilson, "in a few parts so bad, and in all parts so unlike what adult readers of our century expect to read, that an honest critic today must surely approach its reputation with skepticism." Nevertheless, concludes Wilson, "it is an exceptional, a truly wonderful book." [50]

The title page of The Posthumous Papers of the Pickwick Club, *also known as* The Pickwick Papers, *published in 1836.*

A major setback occurred while the third issue was in production: Robert Seymour fatally shot himself. Official reports said he suffered from "temporary derangement," but both his publishers and Dickens knew that this condition had existed long before *The Pickwick Papers.* "He was, like many illustrators," writes Peter Ackroyd, "a melancholy and in some ways thwarted man."[51]

Finding a competent illustrator to replace Seymour was not easy, but at last the publishers settled on Hablot Knight Browne, a young man not yet twenty-one, whose drawings complemented Dickens's writing but did little to increase the sales of the next few numbers. By the fifth installment, however, the series began to attract a wide audience; at the end of July Dickens wrote at the bottom of a letter to a friend, actor John Macrone, "PICKWICK TRIUMPHANT."

A Sense of Humor

One of the author's greatest writing strengths was his humor. "To this day," writes Brian Murray, "Dickens's position as the greatest humorist in the English language goes unchallenged."[52] Already in *Pickwick,* his first major work, he blended the winning elements that he would use in many future novels: humor, criticism of social evils and public institutions, encounters with ghostly figures and death, an excellent knowledge of London, and a superb use of the English language. The kindly and caring spirit of many of his characters evoked pity and affection from readers.

The Pickwick Papers made Dickens one of the most popular authors of his day. Unlike his later novels, notes Stephen Leacock, "*Mr. Pickwick* had no theme or moral at all, and did excellently without one."[53]

It was superb characters like Samuel Pickwick, Esquire, who won people's hearts. Pickwick "benignly reigns over all activities of the Pickwick Club, satisfied under every circumstance, that he has helped his fellow creatures by his well-meaning efforts." *Pickwick* was the first major work to focus on the lives and activities of lower- and middle-class citizens. The greatest of these was Sam

Weller, whose "imperturbable presence of mind and his ready wit [were so] indispensable to the Pickwickians."[54]

Joy and Sorrow

The day after the release of *Pickwick*'s first issue, its author married Catherine Hogarth. They moved into rooms at Furnival's Inn in London, where Dickens had lived for two years. As a bachelor he had described Furnival's as "that stronghold of Melancholy,"[55] but the companionship of a wife brightened his feelings for the place. Although it was small, his brother Frederick and Catherine's sister Mary often stayed with them. After one of Mary's visits she told her cousin that Catherine

makes a most capital housekeeper and is as happy as the day is long—I think they are more devoted than ever since

---

What Made *Pickwick* Triumphant?

Edgar Johnson writes in Charles Dickens: His Tragedy and Triumph *that the turning point in* Pickwick *comes in chapter 10, "in which Mr. Pickwick comes upon Sam Weller cleaning shoes in the White Hart Yard and determines to take Sam into his own employ. . . . Mr. Pickwick's discovery of Sam in fact marks the crucial point in* Pickwick's *fortunes." From chapter 10 of the book:*

"It was in the yard of . . . the White Hart that a man was busily employed in brushing the dirt off a pair of boots, early [in] the morning . . . an old white hat was carelessly thrown on one side of his head. There were two rows of boots before him, one cleaned and the other dirty, and at every addition he made to the clean row, he paused from his work, and contemplated its results with evident satisfaction. . . .

A loud ringing of one of the bells, was followed by the appearance of a smart chambermaid in the upper sleeping gallery, who, after tapping one of the doors, and receiving a request from within, called over the balustrades . . .

'Number twenty-two wants his boots.'

'Ask number twenty-two, wether he'll have 'em now, or wait till he gets 'em' was the reply. . . .

There was another loud ring; and the bustling old landlady of the White Hart made her appearance in the opposite gallery.

'Sam,' cried the landlady, 'where's that lazy, idle—why, Sam—oh, there you are; why don't you answer?'

'Wouldn't be gen-teel to answer, 'till you'd done talking,' replied Sam, gruffly."

---

their Marriage if that be possible. . . . He is such a nice creature and so clever he is courted and made up to by all literary Gentlemen, and has more to do in that way than he can well manage.[56]

Mary's assessment of Dickens's workload was correct. The success of *Sketches*, followed by *Pickwick*, put him in demand as a writer. In addition to the articles, he wrote two plays, *The Strange Gentleman* and *The Village Coquettes*, which were produced in London. He also authored a pamphlet supporting the right of the poor to enjoy leisure time activities on the Sabbath, a practice unheard-of in Victorian England.

Among those watching Dickens's ascent was publisher Richard Bentley, a short man and fast talker who soon persuaded

The death of sister-in-law Mary Hogarth (pictured) in 1837 sent Dickens into a deep depression.

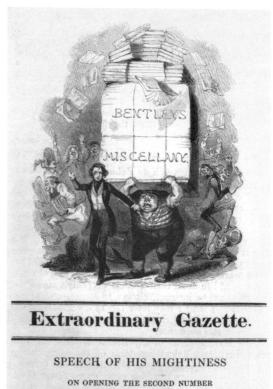

An 1837 advertisement for Bentley's Miscellany *depicts Dickens, the editor, distributing copies of the magazine.*

him to sign a contract for a novel in three volumes. In agreeing, Dickens overextended himself and was forced to cancel several projects, including a novel for his friend Macrone, which caused hard feelings. In November 1836, he resigned from the *Chronicle* to become editor of Bentley's new magazine, *The Wits Miscellany*, soon called *Bentley's Miscellany*.

Dickens tried hard not to let his growing fame take over his personal life. Angus Wilson calls him "a strongly sensual man [with] a deep social and emotional need for family life and love."[57] Dickens enjoyed having children around the house. In anticipation of a family, he and Kate moved to a larger home on Doughty Street, today the Dickens House Museum. There, in January 1837, their first child, Charles Culliford Boz, was born. During Kate's recovery, her sister Mary helped in the house. In a letter to their cousin, Mary wrote that Charles was "kindness itself" to Kate, "constantly studying her in everything. . . . His literary career gets more and more prosperous every day, and he is courted and flattered on every side by all the great folks of this great city."[58]

Grief Stricken

On May 6, Mary attended a play with Charles, Kate, and other family members. When they arrived home, she "went upstairs to bed at about one o'clock in perfect health and her usual delightful spirits." But soon, Charles heard a strange cry coming from her room. Realizing that Mary was severely ill, his brother Frederick ran for a doctor. But the young woman had suffered a heart attack, and there was little the doctor could do. A stricken Dickens, feeling perhaps the deepest grief of his life, later wrote:

She sank under the attack and died— died in such a calm and gentle sleep, that although I had held her in my arms for some time before, when she was certainly living . . . I continued to support her lifeless form, long after her soul had fled to Heaven. . . . You cannot conceive the misery in which this dreadful event has plunged us. Since our marriage she has been the peace and life of our home . . . she has been to us what we can never replace, and has left a blank which no one who ever knew her can have the faintest hope of seeing supplied.[59]

Master Humphrey's Clock

In 1839 Dickens developed the idea for a magazine called Master Humphrey's Clock. *Critic Angus Wilson has little good to say about the project in* The World of Charles Dickens.

"The overworked Charles Dickens thought that he had now seen how to meet the rising cost of his way of living, of his growing family . . . and the ever-swelling number of his dependants. He put before his publishers . . . a scheme for a sort of *Arabian Nights Entertainment* of Dickens fiction. It was, it must be confessed, a lazy scheme of an overpressed young man in which he hoped to use the popularity of Mr. Pickwick and Sam Weller all over again; and in which a quaint old narrator, Master Humphrey, should link a series of stories."

Oliver Twist

Dickens's deep sadness was tempered by the promise of an exciting future. While working on the second issue of the magazine, he wrote Bentley, "I am very happy to say that I think the next No. will be an exceedingly good one. I have bestowed great pains and time upon it, and shall consider the arrangement well. Moreover, I think I have hit on a capital notion for myself, and one which will bring [the illustrator George] Cruikshank out."[60]

Dickens's grand new idea was the beginning of *Oliver Twist*, one of the most popular novels in the English language. Oliver, the orphan boy caught up by a band of London thieves, would become—along with Dracula and Huckleberry Finn—one of the best known of all fictional characters. For two years, from February 1837 to April 1839, *Oliver Twist* ran monthly in *Bentley's*. As Dickens had predicted, the book brought out some of the best in caricaturist George Cruikshank, who had illustrated *Sketches by Boz*. But Cruikshank likewise brought Dickens's characters and settings to vivid life.

Pickwick had given Dickens the self-assurance he needed to create *Oliver Twist*, but while he was working on *Oliver*, he was also finishing installments of *Pickwick*. His tremendous energy made him one of the most prolific writers of his time. Not only was he turning out a great deal of good material, he was trying different styles, subjects, and themes.

Like many of Dickens's most successful characters, Oliver was a simple person, without complex goals, who sought an honest life with caring people. The book's theme—the anguish of a neglected child-hood—is also simple and practical, filled with social criticism. The novel is harsh on London: Dickens explained why: "The amount of crime, starvation and nakedness and misery of every sort in the metropolis surpasses all understanding. . . . I have spent many days and nights in the most wretched districts . . . studying the history of the human heart. There we must go to find it."[61] One of those places, says Peter Ackroyd, was Folly Ditch, a creek or inlet of the Thames, described in *Oliver Twist*:

> The backs of half-a-dozen houses, with holes from which to look upon the slime beneath; windows, broken and patched, with poles thrust out, on which to dry the linen that is never there; rooms so small, so filthy, so confined, that the air would seem too tainted even for the dirt and squalor which they shelter; . . . every repulsive lineament of poverty, every loathsome indication of filth, rot, and garbage; all these ornament the banks of Folly Ditch.[62]

Dickens the Family Man

Dickens had great empathy for the children of London as well as for the poverty stricken. "In 1839," notes Piers Dudgeon, "almost half the funerals in London were children under ten years of age. Most occurred among the poor and especially among children of working women."[63] His concern is most notably reflected in the death of Little Nell in *The Old Curiosity Shop*.

Dickens's own disrupted childhood made him seek stability in his adult life. In the early years of his marriage, he was a family man, devoted to his wife and home.

Nicholas Nickleby

Charles Dickens in 1839, around the time he wrote Oliver Twist *and* Nicholas Nickleby.

His second child, Mary, was born in 1838, daughter Kate one year later. He enjoyed spending time with the children, and after they were in bed he took long walks on London's streets.

At the same time, he was "an able and strong-minded man," wrote the *Times* of London, "who would have succeeded in almost any profession to which he devoted himself."[64] Dickens was a social person (except when he faced a writing deadline) and he mixed with a variety of friendly, vibrant people, not just London's literary set. Snobbishness he could not abide; he much preferred the company of down-to-earth, practical people.

To *Oliver Twist*, still in progress, Dickens added another major writing obligation, in addition to assorted lesser commitments:

> My month's work . . . has been dreadful—Grimaldi [an editing job for Bentley], the anonymous book for Chapman and Hall, Oliver, and the Miscellany. They are all done, thank God, and I start on my pilgrimage to the cheap schools of Yorkshire (a mighty secret of course) next Monday Morning.[65]

The pilgrimage to the cheap schools was in preparation for his new work, *Nicholas Nickleby,* a critique of British boarding schools. These schools were notorious not only for failing to educate students but for abuse, neglect, and even death. Since his childhood in Chatham, Dickens had heard the horrible story of a boy who had come home with an infected abscess "in consequence of his [schoolmaster] having ripped it open with an inky pen-knife."[66] Now, in the company of his illustrator, Browne, famously known as Phiz, he set out to explore such conditions firsthand.

Unfortunately the schoolmasters of Yorkshire suspected their purpose, and the pair gained little firsthand knowledge. "But Dickens had seen all he needed," writes Ackroyd. "It is probable that all along he knew approximately how he would deal with the subject."[67] For the novel, he created an academy run by the notorious Wackford Squeers, "a school where boys were not taught a thing, but were simply whipped, starved, and cowed in order to keep their spirits and the proprietor's expenses down."[68] The hero, Nicholas, recently hired by the school,

In an illustration from Dickens's Nicholas Nickleby, *Ralph (Nicholas's uncle) entertains clients in his office.*

spends the first night on a dormitory floor with the boys in his charge:

> As they lay closely packed together, covered, for warmth's sake, with their patched and ragged clothes, little could be distinguished but the sharp outlines of pale faces. . . . There were some who, lying on their backs with upturned faces and clenched hands, just visible in the leaden light, bore more the aspect of dead bodies than of living creatures.[69]

Changes in the educational system began to occur after the publication of *Nicholas Nickleby* on April 1, 1838. Dickens was delighted by reports that the headmasters of several schools were threatening lawsuits against him for what they consid-

ered defamation of character and that of their schools. "It has been claimed," said one report, "that to Dickens alone can be given the credit for arousing the wave of indignation that forced many institutions to close or to change."[70]

John Forster: Dickens's Lifelong Confidant

Upon his return from Yorkshire and his twenty-sixth birthday, Dickens wrote to his friend John Forster: "I *have* begun! I wrote four slips [short pages] last night, so you see the beginning is made . . . the book is in training at last." On February 9 he reported, "The first chapter of Nicholas is done."[71]

John Forster was one of Dickens's closest companions and confidants. They met in the winter of 1836 and, despite periodic quarrels, kept a close friendship throughout their lives. When Forster's brother died, Charles wrote him, "You have a Brother left. One bound to you by ties as strong as ever Nature forged. By ties never to be broken, weakened, changed in any way." [72]

A writer, reviewer, and journalist, Forster was a notable figure in literary London. His writing talent and legal background made him agent and adviser to many leading writers of the day. He was "pompous but loyal," [73] according to biographer Brian Murray. In his exhaustive biography *Life of Dickens* (1872–1874), Forster proclaims his friend "the most popular novelist of the century, and one of the greatest humorists that England has produced." [74]

Dickens, for his part, relied heavily on Forster's judgment and friendship. On his first trip to America, a separation of several months, he wrote, "How I miss you. . . . How seriously I have thought many, many times . . . of the terrible folly of ever quarrelling with a true friend." [75]

It was Forster who advised Dickens on one of his greatest plot quandaries, which arose in his next novel, *The Old Curiosity Shop*. Published in installments from 1840 to 1841, the book is not considered one of Dickens's best. It is, however, one of his best known for the character of orphan Nell Trent, the much loved granddaughter of a kindly old gentleman who ran a local curiosity shop.

Nell represents the thousands of London children whom Dickens pitied as the victims of society's ills. Despite her

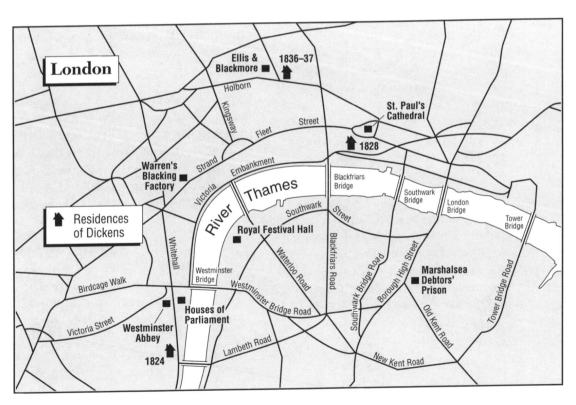

The house at No. 1 Devonshire Terrace in London, where Dickens lived while he wrote The Old Curiosity Shop, Barnaby Rudge, A Christmas Carol, Martin Chuzzlewit, Dombey and Son, *and* David Copperfield.

grandfather's gambling habit, Nell is devoted to him. She protects and defends him, in the end sacrificing her health in their escape from the hated creditor Quilp. Grandfather is with the child as she is dying:

> "Why dost thou lie so idle there, dear Nell," he murmured, "when there are bright red berries out of doors waiting for thee to pluck them! Why does thou lie so idle there, when thy little friends come creeping to the door, crying 'Where is Nell—sweet Nell?' and sob, and weep, because they do not see thee!"...

> Her couch was dressed with here and there some winter berries and green leaves, gathered in a spot she had been used to favour. "When I die, put near me something that has loved the light, and had the sky above it always." Those were her words.

> She was dead. Dear, gentle, patient, noble Nell was dead. Her little bird—a poor slight thing the pressure of a fin-

ger would have crushed—was stirring nimbly in its cage; and the strong heart of its child mistress was mute and motionless forever. [76]

Originally Dickens had not planned Nell's death, but Forster proved a strong influence:

> When Forster suggested that her death would be the appropriate resolution to the novel, [Dickens] realized that, instinctively, unconsciously, he had from the beginning made that [decision]. . . . Forster advised him to do only what he already knew had to be done. [77]

A reflection of Dickens's grief over the death of Mary Hogarth, Nell's death is one of the most poignant in all literature. Dickens's critics cried "Victorian sentimentality," which they claimed was his greatest weakness. Nevertheless, the book made him even more popular at home and gained for him a whole new continent of fans: the Americans.

4 "Unbounded Praise, Unstinted Hospitality"

> Dickens's spirits soared like a balloon. . . . [His] contagious gaiety bubbled . . . like flowing champagne.
>
> —Edgar Johnson, *Charles Dickens*

After *Barnaby Rudge,* Dickens was tired. He needed rejuvenation. So when Chapman and Hall suggested a trip to the United States, with a book to follow, he was enthusiastic. "I am still haunted," he wrote Forster, "by visions of America. . . . Kate cries dismally if I mention the subject. But, God willing, I think it must be managed somehow!"[78]

Heading to America

The Dickens children, now numbering four with the arrival of Walter Landor Dickens in 1841, posed the biggest problem. What was to be done with them while their parents were away in America? At length an arrangement was made for Dickens's brother Fred and an actor friend, William Macready, to share the children's care. This, along with the news that her maid, Anne Brown, would accompany them, made Catherine a bit more enthusiastic about the trip, but she did not share Charles's excitement.

On January 4, 1842, the party set sail from Liverpool to Boston aboard the steamship *Britannia.* It was a terrible trip through a fierce North Atlantic storm. "I never expected to see the day again, and resigned myself to God as well as I could," Dickens wrote Forster. Kate suffered a severe toothache and wretched seasickness the entire trip. After the ship struck a mud bank near Halifax, Nova Scotia, and distress flares were fired, she wrote her sister-in-law, "I was nearly distracted with terror, and don't know what I should have done had it not been for the great kindness and composure of my dear Charles."[79]

Arrival in Boston

Upon docking in the United States, a hectic itinerary awaited Dickens: Boston, New York, Baltimore, Washington, Louisville, St. Louis, Cincinnati, and points between. Their reception in Boston was stupendous. Throngs of people and hordes of reporters followed the author wherever he went. Wrote Dickens in a letter home: "I can give you no conception of my welcome here. . . . There never was a king or emperor upon earth so cheered and followed by crowds and entertained in public at splendid balls

America, as Recorded in Dickens's Letters Home

Dickens poured out his feelings on America in a letter to his friend Macready, reprinted in Johnson's Charles Dickens: His Tragedy and Triumph.

"This is not the republic I came to see; this is not the republic of my imagination. . . . In everything of which it has made a boast—excepting its education of the people and its care for poor children—it sinks immeasurably below the level I had placed it upon."

And yet he remained positive about the American people:

"The people are affectionate, generous, open-hearted, hospitable, enthusiastic, good-humoured, polite to women, frank and candid to all strangers, anxious to oblige, far less prejudiced than they have been described to be, frequently polished and refined, very seldom rude or disagreeable. . . . I have seen none of that greediness and indecorum on which travellers have laid so much emphasis. I have . . . not spoken to one man, woman, or child of any degree who has not grown positively affectionate before we parted."

and dinners and waited upon by public bodies and deputations of all kinds."[80]

Some of America's finest scholars, politicians, and writers greeted the Dickenses in Boston: Richard Henry Dana, Charles Sumner, Henry Wadsworth Longfellow, and others. Charles's enthusiasm for America could not be contained. He had, he said, "dreamed by day and night, for years, of setting foot upon this shore, and breathing this pure air."[81]

On to New York

On February 13, the Dickenses traveled to New York, where they stayed for the next three weeks. Here they met notable writers Washington Irving, William Cullen Bryant, and Fitz-Green Halleck. The mayor and leading citizens framed an official welcome, which read in part: "It is proper and becoming in the citizens of New York to unite heartily in these demonstrations of respect and esteem which have been and will be, everywhere in our land called forth by the visit of Mr. Dickens to America."[82]

"He expected and received unbounded praise, unstinted hospitality, and national publicity,"[83] wrote one historian. The highlight of their stay in New York was the gala Boz Ball, held at the Park Theatre with room to accommodate three thousand dancers. "If he does not get his head turned by all this, I shall wonder at it,"[84] wrote one of the organizers. The affair left Charles in bed for four days with a wretched sore throat.

A Growing Disenchantment with America

Despite his illness, he was the featured speaker at a banquet for more than 230 male guests, among whom were many authors and publishers. To them Dickens raised "a question of universal literary interest"[85] that caused controversy on his American tour. The subject was international copyright protection. Dickens took issue with the American publishing practice of reprinting the works of popular foreign authors without paying them a royalty.

Newspapers bristled at his outspokenness, calling the creator of poor, orphaned Oliver Twist "a greedy charlatan and an ungrateful guest."[86] Wrote the Hartford, Connecticut, *Times*, "It happens that we want no advice on the subject and it will be better for Mr. Dickens if he refrains from introducing the subject hereafter."[87]

But Dickens could not refrain. His copyright grievance and his exhausting schedule of public appearances caused his bright view of America to dim. After ten days in New York he wrote Jonathan Chapman, "I am sick to death of the life I have

A ticket to the Boz Ball, held in honor of Charles Dickens during his stay in New York. The event took place in a ballroom large enough to accommodate three thousand dancers.

been leading here—worn out in mind and body—and quite weary and distressed." To Forster he confided, "I can do nothing that I want to do, go nowhere where I want to go, and see nothing that I want to see. . . . I have no rest or peace, and am in a perpetual worry."[88]

Actually, it was not quite that bad. Dickens, always a lover of the spotlight, found many aspects of American life to his liking. In Boston he found the public prisons and asylums "efficient and humane."[89] Nor was the American press constantly critical: Dickens, wrote one journalist, was surrounded by an aura of extraordinary life and potential.

By the time they left for Philadelphia on March 8, Kate was hopelessly homesick.

America, as Recorded in *American Notes*

Angus Wilson says in The World of Charles Dickens *that* American Notes, *the collection of essays that resulted from Dickens's trip to America, was, on the whole*

"pretty dull reading . . . so that a careless reader could not be blamed if he thought that the American nation consisted mainly of convicts, with a sprinkling of the destitute, lunatics, blind people and the deaf and dumb."

Because of Dickens's unfavorable impressions of American life, there were some people, writes Edgar Johnson in Charles Dickens: His Tragedy and Triumph, *"who were seriously perturbed at what [he] might write [in a book]." Dickens was "keenly aware of the angry reception the book would have throughout most of the American press," but he was determined not to whitewash his feelings:*

"He therefore planned . . . an introductory chapter outlining his position. [In it he said that] the book . . . was not statistical. It avoided personalities. It was not political. It contained no description of the reception "a most affectionate and generous-hearted people" had given him. . . . It was simply a day-by-day record of things that had passed under his eye, with some of his reflections upon them."

"Unfortunately," reports Johnson, "Forster strongly opposed printing this introduction, and in the end Dickens at last allowed himself to be won over." American Notes *greatly needed an explanatory introduction.*

Charles, too, was becoming increasingly displeased with certain aspects of American life. He found the habit of chewing and spitting tobacco horribly revolting. "In every bar-room and hotel passage," he wrote, "the stone floor looks as if it were paved with open oysters—from the quantity of this kind of deposit which tessellates [makes a pattern] all over."[90]

Visiting Slavery Regions

"We are now in the regions of slavery, spittoons, and senators," he commented, as they headed south from Philadelphia toward Washington, "—all three are evils in all countries."[91] Dickens was a firm abolitionist and refused to be waited upon by slaves. He was appalled to see a recently purchased black slave mother and her children riding in the "negro car" on a train. To Forster he wrote, "It is all very well to say 'be silent on the subject [of slavery].' They won't let you be silent. They *will* ask you what you think of it; and *will* expatiate [make excuses for] slavery as if it were one of the greatest blessings of mankind."[92]

In the nation's capital, the Dickenses met many distinguished heads of state, including President John Tyler and former president John Quincy Adams. Charles observed the White House with his usual satirical eye:

A few [of the men] were eyeing the movables as if to make quite sure that the President (who is not popular) hadn't made away with any of the furniture, or sold the fixtures for his private benefit. . . . They all constantly squirted forth upon the carpet a yellow saliva

which quite altered its pattern; and even the few who did not indulge in this recreation, expectorated abundantly.[93]

Points West

Just before they headed west, a letter arrived from Macready, telling them that all was well at home. Their spirits buoyed, especially Kate's, they set off for Ohio, traveling by stagecoach and riverboat, since rail lines had been laid only twelve miles west of Baltimore. Dickens was impressed by the Cincinnati public school system, and he proclaimed the city "very beautiful . . . the prettiest place I have seen here, except Boston."[94]

But their journey by steamboat on the Mississippi River to St. Louis was not so impressive. "The beastliest river in the world," Dickens called it,

a dismal swamp, on which the half-built houses rot away . . . on ground so flat and low . . . a breeding place of fever, ague, and death . . . the hateful Mississippi circling and eddying before it . . . a place without one single quality, in earth or air or water, to commend it.[95]

The westernmost point of their trip was St. Louis, where Dickens asked that he be excused from some social obligations so that he could visit the prairie. He had heard much about this wide, flat land and, in the company of thirteen other travelers, headed for the Looking Glass Prairie. Again his expectations were unfulfilled. It struck him as a lesser version of Britain's Salisbury plain, "a sea without water,"[96] he wrote Forster.

As often happens with homesick travelers, Dickens found that the longer he was away, the greater was his dissatisfaction with American people and customs. Returning east through Ohio, he wrote that the people were "morose, sullen, clownish, and repulsive . . . destitute of humour. . . . I have not heard a hearty laugh these six weeks, except my own."[97]

As they neared the end of their journey, the Dickenses headed north to Canada, where they visited spectacular Niagara Falls. "Nature's greatest altar,"[98] Dickens proclaimed this natural wonder. He especially loved the Canadian side, "when I felt how near to my Creator I was standing."[99]

The Return Home

Because Canada was a British colony, he found there many reminders of home. "English kindness is very different from American,"[100] Dickens wrote upon his arrival. They spent eighteen days in Canada, "the most enjoyable, no doubt, of all his American experience, except perhaps the opening days in Boston."[101] Canadian throngs greeted the Dickenses wherever they went and Charles was constantly obliged to shake hands and sign autographs.

By now, as he wrote Forster, the couple was "fevered with anxiety for home. . . . Kiss our darlings for us. We shall soon meet, please God, and be happier and merrier than ever we were, in all our lives. . . . Oh home—home—home—home—home—home—HOME!!!!!!!!!!!!"[102]

Their discomfort on the steamship to America convinced the Dickenses to return by sailing packet (a swifter, medium-size vessel), and they arrived in England on June 29. "The pleasures of home," he

America, as Recorded in *Martin Chuzzlewit*

In Martin Chuzzlewit, *Dickens's main character travels to America. Martin disembarks at the port of New York and, before reaching land, is greeted by throngs of reporters like those whom Dickens found so irritating and overbearing on his own tour.*

" 'Let me ask you, sir . . . how do you like my Country?'

'I am hardly prepared to answer that question,' said Martin, 'seeing that I have not been ashore.'. . .

'You have brought, I see sir,' [the reporter] said, turning round towards Martin, . . . 'the usual amount of misery and poverty and ignorance and crime, to be located in the bosom of the great Republic [America]. Well, sir! Let 'em come on in ship-loads from the old country [England]. When vessels [the British government] are about to founder, the rats are said to leave 'em. There is considerable of truth, I find, in that remark.'

'The old ship [England] will keep afloat a year or two longer yet, perhaps,' said Martin with a smile."

The four eldest Dickens children: Katey, Walter, Charley, and Mamie. Dickens took a great interest in his children and especially enjoyed spending the holidays with them.

told Jonathan Chapman, "are unspeakable. . . . I never in my life felt so keenly as on the night of our reaching it."[103]

Home Again, Home Again

The two to three years following the Dickenses' return were some of the best of their lives. During this time two more children were born, Francis Jeffrey and Alfred Tennyson. Catherine's sister Georgina moved in with the family to help care for the children and remained in the home until Dickens's death. Charles loved a household full of young children and gave each of them nicknames, as he might name literary characters. Francis was "Chickenstalker"; Alfred was "Sampson Brass" or "Skittles."

Although he enjoyed cooking well enough to consider writing a cookbook, Dickens's daughter Mary recalled that he was "the most abstemious [moderate in drinking and eating] of men, that he rarely ate anything of consequence for luncheon, and that his pleasure was rather in planning and ordering a dinner than in eating it."[104] The Dickens home was, for the moment, a comfortable, secure place:

The shadows that were to come later as yet [had not] fallen across the threshold of his home. At this period of his life he had not yet undertaken the burden of overwork which ultimately broke him down. The endless toil of his editorial years had not yet begun.[105]

5 The Highest Reach of His Achievement

Christmas in his own home, with his own family, was a peak celebration of high spirits and good will for Dickens.

—Angus Wilson,
The World of Charles Dickens

The instability of his own childhood made Charles Dickens cherish the love, warmth, and peace of Christmas, and wish that it would last throughout the year. At the center of this idealized image was a close family scene that "bound together all our home enjoyments, affections and hopes."[106] Says biographer Peter Ackroyd, "It might seem that in the glowing accounts of these seasonal festivities in his fiction he is trying to revive the benevolence [goodwill] of his lost childhood."[107] Children were central to Dickens's image of Christmas, writes author Frank Donovan: "There was a connection in Dickens's thinking between the spirit of Christmas and the spirit of childhood, in that both placed spiritual above material values; both placed high value on love . . . as a necessity for a happier life."[108]

Although he published a Christmas story every year from 1843 to 1867 except 1847, the only one widely known is the much loved *A Christmas Carol.* Dickens claimed it was "tossed off" in a few weeks while writing his larger work *Martin Chuzzle-*

wit. Published in December 1843, the *Carol* was expensive to produce and poorly advertised, and at first it did not sell well. Today, critics have called it the second-greatest Christmas story every written, after the biblical account of the Nativity in the Gospel of Matthew.

The fantastical tale of the miserly Ebenezer Scrooge, who renounces his cold-hearted materialism for love and compassion after being visited by a series of ghosts on Christmas Eve, *A Christmas Carol* accomplished two great missions. One was to show that "Christmas can and should bring love and brotherhood into the life of man." The other was to expose "the callous attitude of the English mercantile [merchant] system toward the poor and underprivileged."[109]

A Year on the Continent

After a disappointingly slow start, the January 1 sales reports on the *Carol* at last brought hope to the author. Encouraged by rising sales figures, Dickens promised himself and his family "a glorious year of freedom in France, Italy, perhaps Germany!"[110] In Italy, Dickens hoped, the lower costs of living would improve his fi-

In a scene from A Christmas Carol, *Tiny Tim is carried home on the shoulder of his father.*

nancial status. He also hoped the break would be a cooling-off period in an increasingly strained relationship with his publishers, Chapman and Hall.

The Dickens party traveled first to France, then to Genoa, Italy, which became their home for a year. Although they enjoyed Italy and were accorded the royal treatment Dickens was now used to receiving, the author never felt at home there. A letter to Forster reveals his homesickness for some of the old, familiar landmarks of London:

> I seem as if I had plucked myself out of my proper soil when I left Devonshire Terrace. If the fountains here played

nectar they wouldn't please me half as well as the Middlesex waterworks at Devonshire Terrace. Put me down on Waterloo Bridge at eight o'clock in the evening, with leave to roam about as long as I like, and I would come home as you know, panting to go on.[111]

Despite his homesickness, he was soon hard at work on another Christmas story, inspired by memories of London. He kept careful notes of his impressions of Italy, published in 1846 as *Pictures from Italy*, a book with few passages worth noting or quoting. In June 1845, after a year on the Continent, the family returned to London, crossing the Swiss Alps by carriage, then passing through Belgium and across the Channel to England.

A Brief Diversion in Acting and Editing

Upon his return, Dickens embarked on one of his few misguided professional endeavors. The fiasco was the launching of a liberal newspaper he would edit himself, a forum for his views on issues such as educational reform, opposition to an alcoholic abstinence campaign, and elimination of public hangings.

Many of Dickens's closest advisers, including Forster, opposed the newspaper idea. His former publishers, Bradbury and Evans, supported the project, however, and on January 21, 1846, the first issue of the *Daily News* appeared. With his usual zeal for any new undertaking, Dickens "threw his whole soul into it."[112]

Within a week, however, Dickens's soul was out of the newspaper business. Within

Charles Dickens plays the role of Captain Babadil in the play Every Man in His Humour. *Many people in London admired Dickens as much for his acting as for his writing.*

three weeks, his body had followed. He realized that with the "Daily Noose," as he called it, he had taken on a much larger commitment than he could handle, and one that was not particularly to his liking. He found the operation of a newspaper filled with "tedious detail, infinite vexation, and the unanticipated frustration of problems with incompetent printers and nervous investors whose commitment to give him complete control over personnel was not fully honored."[113]

Dickens did serialize his *Pictures from Italy* in the paper, and the *Daily News* pros-

pered for many years, but without his editorial guidance.

What he did much better than edit the *News* was act on the stage. Many considered Dickens the best amateur actor in London. During his life he had roles in twenty major plays and saw his own works performed on the stage. At times as many as twenty theaters were running a Dickens production. Yet despite the success of the theatricals, Dickens was troubled by the fact that he had not been working on a novel since the completion of *Martin Chuzzlewit* nearly two years earlier. Forster and his publishers were anxious for him to get back to his writing. To clear his mind for a new project, Dickens decided that he needed to go abroad again.

Catherine did not want to return to Genoa, so the family went to Lausanne, Switzerland, arriving on June 11, 1846. There Dickens wrote the next Christmas story, *The Battle of Life*, and began work on a new novel, *Dombey and Son*. The Dickenses enjoyed Switzerland, but by mid-November, wintry weather had driven them west to Paris. Here Dickens continued to work on *Dombey and Son*, illustrated by Phiz.

From the first installment, it was a wild success, but Dickens's joy was tempered by distressing news. His favorite sister, Fanny, had consumption and was not expected to live more than a few years, even with the best care. Deeply grieved, Charles decided that the family should return to London at the end of March 1847. Back home another child, Sydney Smith, nicknamed Ocean Spectre, was born on April 14.

A Crucial Novel in Dickens's Development

Charles's grief over his sister's condition shone clearly in *Dombey and Son*. Well-

---

The Pathos of Paul's Death

Some critics felt that Dickens bled his readers' emotions too much with grief-filled scenes of death. But they seemed drawn to such scenes rather than repulsed by them. Dombey and Son *contains an example: As young Dombey lies dying, his older sister, who has taken the place of their own dead mother, comes to his bedside, and the boy speaks movingly to her.*

"Sister and brother wound their arms around each other, and the golden light came streaming in, and fell upon them, locked together.

'How fast the river runs, between its green banks and the rushes, Floy! But 'tis very near the sea. I hear the waves! They always said so!'

Presently he told her that the motion of the boat upon the stream was lulling him to rest. How green the banks were now, how bright the flowers growing on them, and how tall the rushes! Now the boat was out at sea, but gliding smoothly on. And now there was a shore before him. Who stood on the bank!—

He put his hands together, as he had been used to do at his prayers. He did not remove his arms to do it; but they saw him fold them so, behind her neck.

'Mama is like you, Floy. I know her by the face! But tell them that the print upon the stairs at school is not divine enough. The light about the head is shining on me as I go!'"

---

known author William Makepeace Thackeray called the chapter in which young Paul Dombey dies "stupendous" and "unsurpassed." "There's no writing against such power as this," he admitted. "One has no chance!"[114]

For the first time in his career, Dickens developed a plan for the book before he started writing. Such structuring would become a part of his future novels. In *Dombey and Son* he delved deeper than ever before into moral issues and social problems. Critic Kathleen Tillotson called it "[an] uneasiness about contemporary society."[115] The book's message paralleled that of American author Henry David Thoreau, who wrote about the same time: "This world is a place of business. . . . It is nothing but work, work, work. . . . There is nothing, not even crime, more opposed to poetry, to philosophy, and to life itself, than this incessant business."[116]

The Autobiographical Masterpiece

Before *Dombey* was completed, Dickens's soul was stirred by the urge to write an autobiographical work. The memories that swirled around him during the summer and fall of 1848 left one uncertainty in his mind: "whether I shall turn out to be the hero of my own life."[117] Yet despite a wealth of memories, Dickens found it difficult to get started on the book. Another child, Henry Fielding, was about to be born and he was excessively worried about Kate's health. But after writing to Forster that he felt "deepest despondency, as usual, in commencing"[118] he threw himself into the project, *David Copperfield*, and by mid-April 1849 was at the end of the second chapter.

Although *David Copperfield* was some of Dickens's finest writing, initial sales were disappointing. Still he persevered, and by October 21 was able to write Forster:

> I am within three pages of the shore [end]; and am strangely divided, as usual in such cases, between sorrow and joy. . . . If I were to say half of what Copperfield makes me feel to-night, how strangely, even to you, I should be turned inside out! I seem to be sending some part of myself into the Shadowy World.[119]

Dickens put the intimacies of his soul into the character of David, and it was natural that he would feel sad on completion of

A scene from David Copperfield *illustrates Mr. Micawber familiarizing young David with London.*

The Deaths of Ham and Steerforth

The shipwreck scene from Dickens's David Copperfield *is often cited as the most powerful. Ham is killed trying to save a survivor clinging to the mast. Although he does not know it, the victim on the mast is his rival, the deceitful Steerforth. David describes the scene.*

"At length [Ham] neared the wreck. He was so near, that with one more of his vigorous strokes he would be clinging to it,—when a high, green, vast hill-side of water, moving on shoreward, from beyond the ship, he seemed to leap up into it with a mighty bound, and the ship was gone!

Some eddying fragments I saw in the sea, as if a mere cask had been broken, in running to the spot where they were hauling in. Consternation was in every face. They drew him to my very feet—insensible—dead. He was carried to the nearest house; and, no one preventing me now, I remained near him, busy, while every means of restoration were tried; but he had been beaten to death by the great wave, and his generous heart was stilled for ever."

the project. David is the strength of the novel and yet, strangely, Stephen Leacock points out, "There is . . . no such person. David is merely the looking glass in which we see the other characters, the voice through which they speak. . . . [He] has no more character than a spiritualist medium."[120]

It was the childhood chapters that won *Copperfield* its great popularity. The whole book was an enchanting break from heavy social concerns. Comments one critic, "There is in it very little of the dense dark complications which take the place of a plot in the later books."[121] Over the years, Dickens had become increasingly concerned with the evil in the world, but in *Copperfield* his basic optimism about life overshadows those concerns.

By the time the last installment appeared in 1850, the book was a success, and today it is considered by many to be his finest work. Dickens himself shared that opinion: "Like all fathers, I have a favourite child and his name is David Copperfield."[122]

Trial and Tragedy

During the writing of *David Copperfield*, further gloom descended on the Dickens household. After Dora Annie was born on August 16, 1850, Catherine fell into a severe depression, accompanied by anxiety and paranoia, which left her, as Dickens reported, "exceedingly unwell."[123] Her condition was complicated by the illness in February 1851 of little Dora—namesake of the *David Copperfield* heroine—who nearly died of what was called "congestion of the brain." In addition, Dickens's father, John, was suffering from a severe bladder problem.

Dickens was rehearsing a new play, *Not So Bad as We Seem*, when he got word

Landmarks in Dickens's London

London's waterways, particularly the Thames River, played an important role in many of Dickens's plots. Both he and his characters knew the river intimately and its effects on the city's moods. In The Uncommercial Traveller, *a series of personal essays published in 1860, he wrote:*

"The river had an awful look. . . . The wild moon and clouds were as restless as evil conscience in a tumbled bed, and the very shadow of the immensity of London seemed to lie oppressively upon the river."

Southwark Bridge, one of the many avenues across the Thames, was the "iron bridge" that often served as the meeting place in Little Dorrit, *published in 1857. Famed London Bridge, another landmark in the novels, was called the "stone bridge." Even in Dickens's time, a crush of merchants and businessmen crowded the bridges at the beginning and end of the workday. In* Our Mutual Friend, *one of his last novels, he describes a Victorian Age rush hour at London Bridge: "The set of humanity outward from the City is as a set of prisoners departing from gaol [jail]."*

An engraving shows Southwark Bridge in London. London's waterways are often depicted in Dickens's works.

that his father was gravely ill and not expected to survive required surgery. In fact John did survive the painful surgery, which was performed without anesthetic, in characteristic good spirits, but died a short time later, on March 29, 1851. Dora, who had been recovering well from her illness in February, died suddenly on April 14. The Dickens family was mired in grief.

Household Words

After a lengthy period of mourning that was particularly difficult for Kate, Charles was at last able to write, "I am quite happy again, but I have undergone a great deal."[124] In the midst of personal tragedies, Dickens was immersed in a new endeavor, a weekly magazine that combined fiction, features, travel writing, and social criticism. Created with the help of a highly industrious partner, W. H. Wills, the magazine was in part an answer to critics' requests for Dickens's "natural, easy, Pickwickian style" of writing. The critics were rewarded, and *Household Words* became a major success. In the first issue, published March 30, 1850, Dickens promised that the magazine would be "[the] comrade and friend of many thousands of people, of both sexes, and of all ages and conditions. [It will bring] into innumerable homes, from the stirring world around us, the knowledge of many social wonders, good and evil."[125]

Household Words contained installments of Dickens's one sojourn into children's writing. Beginning January 25, 1851, his *Child's History of England* ran (irregularly) for nearly three years, until December 10, 1853. Dickens used a storyteller's way with words to enliven the subject matter of his history. This passage from chapter 16, "England Under Edward the First, Called Longshanks" is typical:

> And now we come to Scotland, which was the great and lasting trouble of the reign of King Edward the First.
>
> About thirteen years after King Edward's coronation, Alexander the Third, the King of Scotland, died of a fall from his horse. He had been married to Margaret, King Edward's sister. All their children being dead, the Scottish crown became the right of a young Princess, only eight years old, the daughter of Eric, King of Norway, who had married a daughter of the deceased sovereign. King Edward proposed, that the Maiden of Norway, as this Princess was called, should be engaged to be married to his eldest son; but, unfortunately, as she was coming over to England she fell sick, and landing on one of the Orkney Islands, died there.[126]

Nearly a century later, critic Stephen Leacock wrote: "[*A Child's History*] is now dead, but it deserves resurrection. It is almost forgotten, but it ought not to be. . . . In some senses, it is the most notable history of England that was ever written."[127]

Chapter

6 Bobbing Up Corkwise from a Sea of Hard Times

This is one of what I call my wandering days before I fall to work. . . . I seem to be always looking at such times for something I have not found in life, but may possibly come to a few thousands of years hence, in some other part of some other system. God knows.

—Dickens, during the writing of *Bleak House*, July 1852

By the mid–nineteenth century, London was moving into the industrial age, becoming less rural and more urban. Advancements in technology such as the steam engine and the railroads, plus improved productivity in the factories, signaled a modern new world. Social advancements were far less impressive. The new, industrialized London was a city of higher crime that did little to protect its children, help its poor, operate a just legal system, or effectively educate its middle and lower classes.

The Ragged Schools were a particularly glaring example of a social ill. These institutions, set up in the slums to help educate poor children, were described by historian Edgar Johnson as "subjected to raids from young hoodlums who pelted the teachers with filth and smashed furniture." Dickens visited one such school and proclaimed it "an awful sight."[128]

Such deplorable social conditions gave Dickens a negative impression of the grand industrial revolution. Dozens of problems were not getting better with time. He had touched upon these evils in earlier novels, the workhouse in *Oliver Twist*, for example. Now he was preoccupied with them and vowed to make them the focus of his writing. It was in this mood that he started *Bleak House*, the first novel whose characters are secondary to the author's social criticism. The novel began serialization in *Household Words* in November 1851.

Dickens's dark social outlook was compounded by a growing frustration with Catherine, who, says biographer Norman MacKenzie, "took little exercise and indulged herself in food and drink." She irritated him, says MacKenzie, "with her lethargy, nervousness, clumsiness, and complaints [and] as the years passed she became more isolated and neglected." His irritation was heightened by Catherine's announcement in the spring of 1852 that another baby was on the way. When Edward Bulwer-Lytton, "Plorn," was born on March 13, Dickens confided to his longtime friend, Miss Angela Coutts, that he had a seventh son "whom I cannot afford to receive with perfect cordiality, as on the whole I could have dispensed with him."[129]

An illustration depicts young schoolgirls crowded inside a London Ragged School. Such London institutions inspired Dickens's darker novels, including Bleak House.

In the hope of restoring his good humor, his doctor recommended a change of scene. Charles and his family moved to Boulogne, France, on June 12, 1853. Here he completed *Bleak House*, a book in which the sarcasm is much harsher and the humor less prevalent than in his early fiction. Dickens's state of mind was clearly reflected in the book's title.

Published in installments by Bradbury and Evans through 1853, *Bleak House* satirized Britain's legal system. Through the fictional lawsuit of *Jarndyce vs. Jarndyce*, Dickens criticized the outrageous amount of time litigation took in the courts. "For many people," writes Stephen Leacock, "*Bleak House* is the most impressive of all Dickens's stories."[130] Other critics have called it "a powerful but confusing novel," and complained that "the plot was weak, that the device of two distinct narrators made for muddled construction, and that the humour was deficient. Dickens was also criticized for his habit of exaggerating physical defects into points of character."[131]

Hard Times

Despite his overtaxed body, mind, and schedule, Dickens lost little time between the completion of *Bleak House* and the start of another dark novel. He began *Hard Times*, his shortest book, on April 1, 1854, and completed it just six months later.

A Harsh Assessment of *Hard Times*

Critics could not agree on the merits of Hard Times. *Thomas Carlyle, whose writings Dickens treasured and to whom he dedicated the book, considered it excellent. John Ruskin, another British writer and critic, said it was in many ways the greatest of Dickens's novels. Others disagreed. Among the most critical was biographer Stephen Leacock, who wrote in* Charles Dickens: His Life and Work:

"*Hard Times* has no other interest in the history of letters than that of its failure. At the time [of its publication], even enthusiastic lovers of Dickens found it hard to read. At present [1933] they do not even try to read it. A large part of the book is mere trash; hardly a chapter of it is worth reading today. . . . Not a chapter or a passage in the book is part of Dickens's legacy to the world."

An illustration from Hard Times *depicts a scene between Louisa and her father.*

This time Dickens attacked industrial conditions in England. George Bernard Shaw called *Hard Times*

[a] rising up against civilization itself as a disease, and declaring that it is not our disorder but our order that is horrible; that it is not our criminals but our magnates [important people in business and politics] that are robbing and murdering us; and that [the core of our corruption is] our entire social system.[132]

The book begins with this memorable statement by the strict and heartless schoolmaster Thomas Gradgrind, who believes that there is no room in the world for imagination or creativity:

Now what I want is, Facts. Teach these boys and girls nothing but Facts. Facts alone are wanted in life. Plant nothing else, and root out everything else. You can only form the minds of reasoning animals upon Facts: nothing else will ever be of any service to them. This is the principle on which I bring up my own children, and this is the principle on which I bring up these children. Stick to Facts, Sir![133]

It was a bleak, colorless, money-motivated world society was moving toward, Dickens believed, and he attacked those whom he considered the culprits, chiefly bankers, industrialists, businessmen, and schoolmasters. Despite its attacks on employers and the upper class, *Hard Times* sold very well. During the first ten weeks of its serialization in *Household Words*, the magazine's circulation doubled. By the end of its six-month run, profits had increased fourfold. But such figures did little to boost Dickens's spirits; he remained depressed.

A Loss of Hope and Faith

The faithful Forster was concerned but also irritated by his friend's continued depression and critical outlook. He described 1855 as "a year of much unsettled discontent" for the author. In *Little Dorrit*, which took shape during this unsettled period, Dickens wrote, "I have no present political faith or hope—not a grain," and added that "representative government is become altogether a failure with us, . . . the whole thing has broken down . . . and has no hope in it."[134]

Adding to the "unsettled discontent" of 1855 was the sudden reappearance of Maria Beadnell. On February 10, just as Dickens was preparing to leave for Paris for a week with a friend, a letter from her arrived. Instantly his longing for her returned, even though the letter made it clear that she was married with children. Immediately he wrote to suggest a meeting upon his return. He asked if she had read *David Copperfield* and recognized in Dora "a faithful reflection of the passion I had for you, and in little bits of 'Dora' touches of your old self sometimes."[135]

The first meeting was a private visit between the two; later Maria and her husband would go to the Dickens's home for dinner. But the reunion was a tremendous disappointment for Charles. Maria was fat at forty-four. What had once been charming, flirtatious mannerisms now seemed awkward and grotesque in a frumpy, middle-aged woman.

After the first meeting, Charles preferred to cancel dinner, but not wanting to hurt Maria or tarnish the memory of those passion-filled days, he kept the date. It was an uneventful evening of mindless chatter

Charles Dickens's house at Gad's Hill. Dickens first dreamed of purchasing Gad's Hill as a child.

with Maria's rather characterless merchant husband, Mr. Winter. Maria sent letters suggesting future meetings, but Dickens felt he could not endure them and began avoiding her.

One of the few bright spots following his reunion with Maria was the prospect of purchasing the house of his childhood dreams, Gad's Hill. "I used to look at it," he recalled, "as a wonderful Mansion . . . when I was a very odd little child with the first faint shadows of all my books in my head." [136]

After months of planning and negotiating, he purchased Gad's Hill on March 14, 1856, and the family arrived on June 1 to spend the summer in this home he called "old fashioned, plain, and comfortable." [137]

Little Dorrit

Dickens's agitation found a positive outlet in his writing. While he was traveling in France, he began work on *Little Dorrit*, the book that portrays so vividly the horrid conditions in the Marshalsea prison. William Dorrit, "Father of the Marshalsea," is a thinly disguised John Dickens.

The heroine, Amy Dorrit, represents a new type of juvenile character for Dickens, much more complex than Oliver, Little Nell, or earlier innocent children. Little Dorrit has an adult soul in a child's body, her character carved from the hard times she endured as a child in the Marshalsea.

She and other complex child characters do not find luck coming to their rescue as frequently as did their earlier counterparts.

Little Dorrit is a dark and somber book that grows even darker as the story progresses. And yet, from the first issue in December 1855, it sold better than any of his previous works. While writing it Dickens confessed, "I have been blowing off a little of [the] indignant steam which would otherwise blow me up." In this book, his increasingly pessimistic outlook found several targets. Biographer Edgar Johnson names a few:

In an illustration for Little Dorrit, *Fanny looks at her reflection in a mirror.* Little Dorrit *brought the horror of debtors' prisons and London jails to the public's attention.*

[He] hated the cold-hearted selfishness of the men of wealth. He despised the . . . snobbery of the middle class. He was contemptuous of the corruption and inefficiency of the Government and bitter over the brutal workings of an economic system that condemned the masses of the people to ignorance, suffering, and squalor.[138]

Little Dorrit helped bring to public attention the horror of debtors prisons and the inhumanity of jailing a person indefinitely for being insolvent. Six years after the novel was published, the British government passed the "Bankruptcy Bill," which limited imprisonment for debt to one year.

A Turbulent Time of Life

To combat his restlessness in the period between *Hard Times* and *Little Dorrit*, Dickens had held public readings of his books. At first the readings were free, but as the audiences and their enthusiasm grew in the summer of 1858, he began charging admission. Soon he discovered that he could earn more doing public readings than he could writing, and that the work was much easier. In addition, the readings satisfied his lifelong need to be adored by his public. As his married life deteriorated, he turned increasingly to his public to love and nurture him.

Dickens's theatrical flair made his writings highly performable and his readings very professional. Combining these talents, he decided to write a melodrama—a play emphasizing emotion and plot—based on the Arctic expedition of Sir John Franklin, whose team of explorers died of starvation and hypothermia. The first performance of *The Frozen Deep* was January 6, 1857, paired with a comedy titled *Uncle John*. Three more performances followed its very favorable opening reception, and the queen even requested a special production. Ultimately the play ran for eight weeks, entertaining thousands of delighted viewers.

Trouble at Home

As the play's run neared its end, Dickens began to slip back into deep depression. His own family was the root of much of his discomfort. At last, in a long letter to Forster, he admitted that

> Poor Catherine and I are not made for each other, and there is no help for it.

It is not only that she makes me uneasy and unhappy, but that I make her so too—and much more so. . . . We are strangely ill-assorted for the bond there is between us. God knows she would have been a thousand times happier if she had married another kind of man, and that her avoidance of this destiny would have been at least equally good for us both.[139]

The problem may not have been simple incompatibility, as Dickens's letters implied. In conversations between his daughter Kate and a friend, released long after she and her father were both dead, she said he spoke of "peculiarities" in his wife's behavior and alluded to a mental disorder. Dickens claimed Catherine had confessed to him that she felt unfit for the role of his wife. She was never especially fond of the children, he maintained, and the feeling was mutual.

An Unnecessary Confession

Dickens was worried about how the news of his separation from Catherine would affect his public. Against the advice of many who were close to him, he published a statement in Household Words, *reprinted by Peter Ackroyd in* Dickens:

"Some domestic troubles of mine, of long-standing [have] lately been brought to an arrangement [with] no anger or ill-will. . . . By some means arising out of wickedness, or out of folly, or out of inconceivable wild chance, this trouble has been made the occasion of misrepresentations, mostly grossly false, most monstrous, and most cruel—involving, not only me, but innocent persons dear to my heart."

Dickens had taken his fame too much for granted. Few beyond his friends and closest acquaintances had any inkling of the affair and would have remained in ignorance but for this article. As it was, the story did little but confuse readers who wondered what it was all about.

Dickens's unhappiness was not limited to Catherine herself. It extended to the entire Hogarth family, who, he claimed, would move into his house for extended visits, expecting him to provide their meals while they relaxed and dirtied the place. He confessed to Forster that the skeleton in his domestic closet was becoming a large one.

In May 1858, Charles and Catherine separated. "Nature has put an insurmountable barrier between us," he wrote to his friend Angela Coutts, "which never in this world can be thrown down." In the long letter, he vented his feelings that the marriage had been doomed from the start:

I believe my marriage has been for years and years as miserable a one as ever was made. . . . I believe that no two people were ever created with such an impossibility of interest, sympathy, confidence, sentiment, tender union of any kind between them, as there is between my wife and me. . . . I think she has always felt herself to be at the disadvantage of groping blindly about me, and never touching me, and so has fallen into the most miserable weaknesses and jealousies.[140]

Catherine's jealousies were not unfounded, however. Charles was having an affair with Ellen Ternan, a young actress who played roles in *Uncle John* and *The Frozen Deep*. The eighteen-year-old Ellen "fascinated him, for she fitted precisely into the ideal of lost innocence which had been so frustratingly evoked by Maria [Beadnell]."[141]

Privately his affection for Ellen became intense. Publicly he did not acknowledge it. Not only was such behavior considered scandalous in Victorian England, but Dickens himself had continually promoted family values and high moral standards in his writing. To be seen as hypocritical could destroy his reputation.

Although Catherine and Charles never lived together again, their separation was peaceable and was kept largely private. Catherine took up residence in the Regent's Park section of London with one of her sons; the other children stayed with their father at Gad's Hill. There they were cared for by the ever-faithful Georgina Hogarth, Catherine's sister, whom Dickens called "the best and truest friend man ever had."[142] During the 1860s, he and Ellen traveled together many times, often to France, and his feelings for her lasted until his death.

7 "It Was the Best of Times, It Was the Worst of Times"

The story of our lives, from year to year.

ALL THE YEAR ROUND

—Quote from Shakespeare's *Othello*, adapted as new magazine title

After Dickens's announcement of his separation from Catherine appeared in *Household Words*, his relationship with the magazine's publishers, Bradbury and Evans, deteriorated. When they rejected his offer to buy their share of the magazine, he followed through on his threat to start a competitive publication. For this he turned to his old publishers, Chapman and Hall, and on April 30, 1859, the first issue of *All the Year Round* appeared. It was an instant success, and subsequent issues far outsold *Household Words*, for Dickens was one of the best periodical editors of the day.

A Tale of Two Cities

He ensured the new magazine's success by serializing his next book in it, the historical novel *A Tale of Two Cities*. Set in London and Paris, it is the complicated but intriguing story of the French Revolution from

In an illustration from A Tale of Two Cities, *Sydney Carton looks off into the distance as he ascends the steps of the guillotine.*

1789 to 1793. Although Dickens took much of his research from Thomas Carlyle's history *French Revolution*, many critics claimed he showed only a superficial understanding of events. Others said he was too melodramatic, relying on a complex

Some Classic Dickens Lines

One of the most often quoted Charles Dickens passages is the opening to A Tale of Two Cities. *These lines use antithesis—contrasts, opposites—to convey a sense of upheaval in 1775 London and Paris. Some have said that they also reflect the chaos and antithesis in Dickens's own life during that period.*

"It was the best of times, it was the worst of times, it was the age of wisdom, it was the age of foolishness, it was the epoch of belief, it was the epoch of incredulity, it was the season of Light, it was the season of Darkness, it was the spring of hope, it was the winter of despair, we had everything before us, we had nothing before us, we were all going direct to Heaven, we were all going direct the other way."

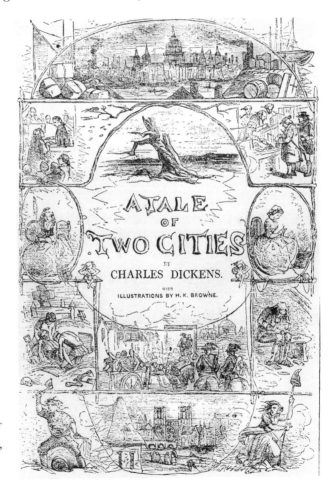

A Tale of Two Cities, *featuring the illustrations of Hablot K. Browne, was printed in London in 1859.*

plot rather than dialogue, character development, and humor. Many critics do not count the book among his major works, saying it lacks too many of Dickens's strengths.

Self-Sacrifice

The theme of self-sacrifice—always important in Dickens's novels—is taken to its highest level in *A Tale of Two Cities*. Sydney Carton, a lawyer's clerk, dies by the guillotine so that his rival, Charles Darnay, can live happily with the woman they both love, Lucie Manette. It was widely speculated that Dickens saw himself as Sydney Carton, wanting to be the hero who made the ultimate sacrifice for Ellen Ternan, the woman he loved.

While he was writing *A Tale of Two Cities*, Dickens maintained an exhausting schedule of public readings. "[His] audiences were quite truly carried away. . . . They laughed, they sobbed, they were in an 'ecstasy,' recalled one observer. Dickens controlled them with hand and voice and eye—like a magician."[143]

Actually, the readings were nearly performances. With his talent for acting, Dickens selected the most "performable" sections of his writings, including scenes from *A Christmas Carol* and the trial from *Pickwick*. One of his most popular readings was "Sikes and Nancy" from *Oliver Twist*, a performance that he honed to dramatic perfection.

The readings were extremely draining. Reviewers called him a human hurricane, claiming that no important author since Homer had put so much time and energy into public performances. By 1860 the readings had taken a great toll on his health, but some of his best writing was yet to come.

Great Expectations

The book that some critics say is Dickens's greatest achievement began running in *All the Year Round* in December 1860. The magazine's sales had been declining and, as usual, a new Dickens serialization improved them.

Great Expectations has perhaps the most powerful opening of any Dickens novel; Pip, the young hero, is accosted by two convicts in a graveyard. In this book Dickens has created immortal characters like those that distinguish his earlier novels. There is Pip, the orphan; the common but kindly Joe Gargery, Pip's brother-in-law; Miss Havisham, an eccentric recluse; the elusive Estella; Magwitch, the convict, who later claims a most unusual tie to Pip; and others. The book criticizes the values of Britain's wealthy and powerful citizens, a criticism that stemmed from Dickens's own impoverished childhood.

The serialization of *Great Expectations* breathed new life into Dickens, but by the completion of the writing he had aged. His physical health and mental state had both deteriorated. Writes biographer Peter Ackroyd:

> He was no longer . . . able to maintain the same rate of composition. He felt himself to be overworking. . . . He was now in his fiftieth year, growing a little bald, unwell, driven by no stern economic necessity but nevertheless driven by something: ". . . I MUST write,"

Estella, one of the main characters from Great Expectations, *stands beside the fireplace in a scene with Miss Havisham.*

were the words he had used in a letter from his country retreat [Gad's Hill], and the chapters he wrote during this period of ill-health, effort and exhaustion are invested with a strange, hallucinatory, murderous tone.[144]

Years of Tragedy

In this period Dickens endured unwelcome changes in his life. As his older friends aged and died, he spent more time with younger ones, but often they were not as creative, educated, or ambitious as the original circle. Those who knew him could tell he was sad and exhausted, nervous and tired.

Alfred, his only brother who had managed to earn a decent living, as an engineer, died of pleurisy, a lung disease, in 1860. When Dickens learned of his death, he knew at once that he would be responsible for Alfred's family. It was not the first time he had been saddled with such responsibility. Wrote Dickens, "[Alfred] left a widow and five children—you may suppose to whom. . . . My mother, who was also left to me when my father died (I never had anything left to me but relations), is in the strangest state of mind from senile decay."[145]

Being much more responsible than his brothers, whom he had long ago renounced for their irresponsible handling of money, Dickens brought Alfred's family to London and helped them reestablish their lives. In the meantime his brother Augustus's wife had lost her eyesight and Augustus had abandoned her to go to America with another woman. Thus Charles was left to support yet another relative.

Jenny and Riah peer through the windows of a toy shop in a scene from Our Mutual Friend. *Critics derided the book, calling it dense and worthless.*

His own children were growing and leaving home, some into unhappy marriages of their own, but there was greater distress in Dickens's life. On September 12, 1863, he wrote to his friend and business partner William Wills, "my poor mother died quite suddenly at last. Her condition was frightful."[146] Three months later his fourth child, Walter Landor, who was deaf, died while traveling in India. Catherine went into deep grief. "Her estranged husband sent out to India an inscription for the boy's tomb, but he sent not one word of condolence to Catherine herself."[147] The separation had made the gap between them permanent and caused friction among their children, some of whom supported their mother and others their father.

During this turbulent period the public's admiration of Dickens remained strong, but the critics were getting harsher. Some people, such as Henry Wadsworth Longfellow and friend John Forster, believed that his last work was his most beautiful. But there were more who insisted that "the books of the decade of the 'sixties . . . cannot rank among the great works of Dickens."[148]

The Pace of Writing Slows

One thing was certain: Dickens's output during the 1860s was below that of previous decades. Still, he worked continuously at editing *All the Year Round* in addition to writing three novels. In the magazine he ran a series of articles collectively titled *The Uncommercial Traveller*. These observations on British life in the 1860s show what one writer calls "Boz in his maturity, roaming about and keenly observing."[149]

Dickens unleashed his growing dissatisfaction with London in two ways. One was his sale of Tavistock House, which meant a permanent move to Gad's Hill, about twenty-five miles southeast of London. "He had come to dislike [the city]," writes Edgar

Johnson, "with its evil-smelling river and the heavy canopy of smoke forever lowering over its housetops."[150] The other was the commencement of a new novel, *Our Mutual Friend*, which attacked the corruption, apathy, and pretensions of Victorian society.

Brian Murray calls *Our Mutual Friend* one of the "more ambitious—and least-readable—novels. . . . Long, dense, and thickly textured, [it] has become one of Dickens's most widely analyzed works. But perhaps most readers will find that it brings sleep not stimulation, and will be hard pressed to slog on much past chapter 5."[151]

Stephen Leacock calls it "interesting only as illustrating the failures of genius. . . . It is in reality of little interest or value except for the interest of asking why it has so little value."[152] Even John Forster was forced to admit "the book will never rank with his higher efforts [for] it wants freshness and natural development."[153]

Despite the criticism, the book is not without merit. Says Murray:

It shows real intellectual ambition, and represents Dickens's deepest (and darkest) thoughts about the corrosive, contaminating effects of life in a culture obsessed with social status and, particularly, money—which is here famously equated with rubbish and dung.[154]

Some readers saw Ellen Ternan in the character of Bella Wilfer, the lovely young woman who was to marry the supposedly murdered John Harmon. Real-life model, or not, Bella is a very believable, well-drawn character—a decided step forward for Dickens, who had perpetual trouble depicting women fully and convincingly. Nevertheless, writes critic Julian Symons, "The characters in his last novels . . . come from the mind of a man defeated, a man possessed [and] are the work of an author who . . . is slowly losing his sense of reality."[155]

Dickens's Major Weaknesses

Many readers who love Dickens's characters have conceded that his plots are poorly conceived and unstructured,

---

Dickens and the Jews

After Dickens was criticized for his treatment of Fagin, the Jew in Oliver Twist, *he responded with a sympathetic character, Riah, in* Our Mutual Friend. *Riah muses:*

"For it is not in Christian countries with the Jews as with other peoples. . . . Men say, 'This is a bad Greek, but there are good Greeks. This is a bad Turk, but there are good Turks.' Not so with the Jews. Men find the bad among us easily enough—among what peoples are the bad not easily found?—but they take the worst of us as samples of the best; they take the lowest of us as presentations of the highest; and they say 'All Jews are alike.'"

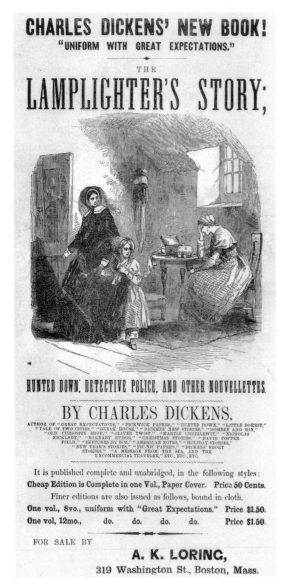

An advertisement for Dickens's The Lamplighter's Story *touts the book as on par with* Great Expectations.

discouraging readers in the first few chapters. In 1865, American novelist Henry James called Dickens "superficial," suggesting that he was in "an inferior rank in the department of letters."[156]

"He Must Have Homage"

Some supporters thought Dickens had fragmented his career with too many nonliterary activities, such as acting, editing, and public readings. They attributed this to his need to be loved by his public. "He must have homage; he must have recognition. Everyone, every single person, must admit that all that he did was wonderful."[157]

By the early twentieth century, as the world sought to distance itself from the prim and proper Victorian era, the opinion of Dickens as a thin and flimsy sentimentalist became even stronger. People grew tired of what they considered simplistic lessons in good versus evil. They wanted literary works that showed more depth, more complex analyses of life. Even George Bernard Shaw, the Irish dramatist who so admired Dickens, admitted that he lacked substance in discussing abstract ideas.

And so, for a time, Dickens's popularity on the world stage dimmed. But this was not permanent. What led him to immortality was his unique ability to weave the subtleties of human behavior, common to all generations, into plots that have not become outdated with the passage of time.

Chapter

8 "I Vanish Now for Evermore"

One can hardly take in the whole truth about it, and feel the universality of his fame.

—American poet Henry Wadsworth Longfellow, on Dickens

During the completion of *Our Mutual Friend* in 1864 and 1865, Dickens frequently traveled to Condette, a small, secluded town in France to which he loved to escape and where he felt his soul renewed. Ellen Ternan and her mother often accompanied him. The May 1865 trip served its usual restorative purpose, but on the return railway trip to London, tragedy struck.

Workmen repairing a bridge near the village of Staplehurst consulted the wrong timetable and were not expecting the 2:38 train from Folkestone. When it appeared, it was too late to stop it and the train derailed, sending all seven first-class cars careening downward. The only car that missed hitting the river was Dickens's, which hung precariously from the bridge.

Dickens rushed to the river to help tend to the dead and dying passengers, having first calmed Ellen and her mother and told them to stay put; until help arrived. At last they were rescued; a train arrived to return the survivors to London, and Dickens collapsed. He spent that night at Gad's Hill, his good friend William Wills in the next room in case he should need something, for the ordeal had left him badly shaken.

Increasing Health Problems

His son later noted that Dickens "may be said never to have altogether recovered" from that disaster. Two years later, the writer himself admitted that the trauma of the accident still affected him: "[It shows] more and more . . . I have sudden vague rushes of terror, even when riding in a hansom cab, which are perfectly unreasonable but quite insurmountable."[158]

After the accident he was plagued by dizzy spells and an uncomfortable swelling in his left foot. He suffered more intensely from gout and arthritis than he had previously, and in the summer of 1866, his doctor diagnosed "degeneration of some functions of the heart."[159]

Dickens was not a man to complain about his health. So when he did admit to friends that his condition was "telling heavily upon me," they took him seriously. "I am nearly used up," he confided to one. Yet in typical Dickens fashion, he prepared to make one of the most exhausting trips

Dickens gives a reading in the United States in 1867. He made the tour despite increasing health problems.

of his career. He planned a reading tour of the United States for 1867. On November 2, shortly before his departure, he was given a gala farewell dinner:

> When Dickens rose shouts stormed upon him. Men leaped on chairs, tossed up napkins, waved glasses and decanters above their heads. The ladies' gallery was a flag of waving fans and handkerchiefs. Colour and pallor followed each other in Dickens's face, and "those wonderful eyes," said one guest, "flamed around like a searchlight"; tears streamed down his cheeks and as he tried to speak his voice faltered.[160]

To America Once Again

Admiration for Charles Dickens in America had remained high, yet many could tell that he was not the person he had been on his earlier tour. One admirer noted that it was like seeing two different people. His American publisher, J. T. Fields, called him the cheeriest man of his age, but the more observant Mrs. Fields noticed that beneath the high spirits lived a sad man.

As he had done twenty-five years earlier, Dickens made Boston his first stop. Public reaction to the readings was overwhelming, and some people paid as much as twenty-five dollars per ticket—at that time a great deal of money. Again, many American literary notables were in the audience. Dickens spent Thanksgiving Day at the home of poet Henry Wadsworth Longfellow.

For the next several weeks, he shuttled between Boston and New York for public readings. In New York, he contracted a cold that turned to a flulike illness. But he refused to quit, and his enchanted audiences seemed not to notice. Despite his health, he headed south to Philadelphia, Baltimore, and Washington. "I have tried allopathy, homoeopathy, cold things, warm things, sweet things, bitter things, stimulants, narcotics, all with the same result. Nothing will touch it,"[161] he reported.

But the show went on. Just days before he was impeached, President Andrew Johnson invited Dickens to the White House. On his birthday, the people of Washington showered him with flowers and greens and "letters radiant with good wishes."[162] He followed that with a rigorous tour of upstate New York, Massachusetts, Connecticut, and Portland, Maine. There he collapsed, and decided to end his tour in April. On April 20, he delivered his last American reading in New York and two days later boarded a boat for home. As it pulled away from the dock, he waved and shouted to his adoring public, "God bless you every one."[163] The American tour had netted him twenty thousand British pounds—a grand sum of money.

Back Home, but Not to Rest

The ocean voyage restored Dickens temporarily, and he arrived home in good spir-

its. Still, he was weakened, and "his shattered health should have warned him against new efforts. He was, and he must have known it, a broken man."[164] But he could not stop; a sort of fatalistic urgency compelled him to continue.

And so he agreed to a hundred-appearance reading tour of the major cities of England and Scotland and vicinities, from October 1868 to May 1869. Those closest to him said he agreed to the tour because he was worried about his children's financial futures. But most of his children were now on their own making reasonable incomes, so his worry may have been part of his unstable mental condition.

The tour began and was, as expected, a great success in its early weeks. Dickens had developed a new performance of the Sikes and Nancy murder scene, which was a sensation. But, "In deciding to add the murder of Nancy to his repertory," writes Edgar Johnson, "he was sentencing himself to death."[165]

In February a continued lameness in his foot prompted his doctors to postpone the readings. A few days later he felt well enough to leave for Scotland, but he soon had another attack. The Sikes and Nancy readings were exhausting, often leaving him prostrate on a couch for hours afterward. On April 17, 1869, at a reading in Chester, his friend Edward Yates reported that Dickens felt lightheaded,

with a tendency to go backwards, and to turn round. Afterwards, desiring to put something on a small table, he pushed it and the table forward, undesignedly. He had some odd feelings of insecurity about his left leg, as if there were something unnatural about his heel . . . some strangeness of his left hand and arm.[166]

These were all signs of an impending stroke, of which Dickens was unaware. Listening at last to his doctors, he took a break in the readings schedule, but was determined to resume the following spring.

The Mystery of Edwin Drood

Dickens spent his enforced rest working on a new novel. Although he was ill and exhausted, a premonition of death likely propelled him into writing with renewed fervor. *The Mystery of Edwin Drood* was very different from his previous works, a murder mystery focusing on the killing of young Edwin Drood by his uncle and guardian, Jack Jasper.

The book is set in Cloisterham, a fictional town based on the real towns of Rochester and Chatham, where Charles lived when he was five, an area known then as "the wickedest place in the world."[167] Dickens loved the cathedral town of Rochester, its grand Christian image transposed against the sinister atmosphere of its opium dens. Jack Jasper, the town choirmaster, was an opium addict. The character of Drood was based on an uncle of Ellen Ternan's, who likewise lit out from Rochester one day, never to be seen again.

It is said that Dickens offered to tell Queen Victoria the book's ending, but that she declined to know and so the world was left to speculate. On one point, scholars did agree: *Edwin Drood* was "the greatest departure from [Dickens's] usual course to be found in any of his novels. Here is neither a broad social panorama like *Chuzzlewit* or *Dorrit*, nor a parable of man's private and social growth like *Copperfield* or *Great Expectations*."[168]

An Affectionate Farewell

Dickens had the first two installments of *Edwin Drood* ready for the printer in late November 1869. Although he regretted having to take time out from his writing, the London "farewell tour" was scheduled to begin in early January, and he needed time to prepare.

The final twelve readings were held in St. James's Hall, where he played to overflow audiences. But his health was fragile. During one of the performances he "found it impossible to say Pickwick, and called him Picksnick, and Picnic, and Peckwicks and all sorts of names except the right [one, giving] a comical glance of surprise"[169] to those in the front row.

But the incident was not comical. It was yet another sign of the heart failure and stroke that would soon claim him. On March 1, Dickens did his final reading from *David Copperfield*. One week later he performed Sikes and Nancy for the last time. Always a physical and emotional drain, this time Dickens vowed, "I shall tear myself to pieces."[170] He did.

The next day, at the queen's request, he appeared at Buckingham Palace for an audience. Although the two had met several years before, they had never talked at length. This time they chatted for an hour, about three times longer than Queen Victoria's usual interviews. "He talked of his latest works, of America, the strangeness of the people there, of the division of classes in England which he hoped would get better in time. He felt sure that it would come gradually."[171]

In her journal, Queen Victoria called Charles Dickens "very agreeable, with a pleasant voice and manner." He, in turn,

The Mystery Within *The Mystery*

The solution to The Mystery of Edwin Drood *remains a mystery. But readers have long pondered what was going through Dickens's mind as he wrote chapter 23, "The Dawn Again," just hours before his death. In that chapter Datchery, a white-haired stranger recently arrived in Cloisterham, rents rooms across from Jack Jasper, young Edwin's guardian. From here, he watches Jasper's every move, including his rendezvous with an old hag selling opium.*

"John Jasper's lamp is kindled, and his Lighthouse is shining when Mr. Datchery returns alone towards it. As mariners on a dangerous voyage, approaching an iron-bound coast, may look along the beams of the warning light to the haven lying beyond it that may never be reached, so Mr. Datchery's wistful gaze is directed to this beacon, and beyond."

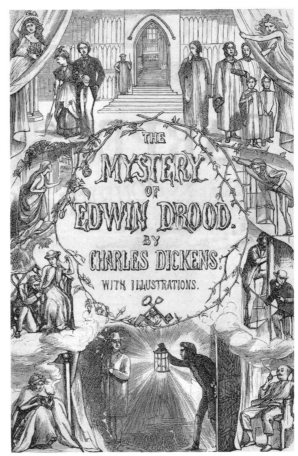

The title page from The Mystery of Edwin Drood. *The book remained unfinished at the time of Dickens's death.*

Dickens's Secret of Productivity

How did Dickens juggle the demands of becoming a successful novelist, conceiving and editing various magazines, supporting an active and successful stage career, and rearing ten children? He managed by budgeting his time very, very carefully, says biographer Brian Murray.

"[His] productivity suggests that Dickens had become a sort of Victorian Isaac Asimov, roped to his desk, his life focused almost entirely on his editing duties and the writing of books. Nothing could be less true. Dickens was prolific [highly productive] because his power of discipline matched his power of imagination; over the years he stuck to a strict routine that limited his writing to one well-defined segment each day. . . . Undoubtedly, Dickens's decision not to hole up in his study but to stay active in his world contributed much to his success."

Dickens sits brooding over a manuscript in his study at Gad's Hill.

found her to be "strangely shy . . . like a girl in manner." Thus, wrote Peter Ackroyd, "did the two greatest representatives of the Victorian era address one another, just as if they were unaware of their place in the history of their time."[172]

On March 15, Charles Dickens gave his final reading at St. James's. Between the United States and Britain he had now delivered 470 readings, and they had nearly cost him his life. He concluded the last one with a tearful farewell in which he admitted:

[I close] this episode in my life with feelings of considerable pain. For some fifteen years, in this hall and in many kindred places, I have had the honour of presenting my own cherished ideas before you for your recognition; and, in closely observing your reception of them, have enjoyed an amount of artistic delight and instruction which, perhaps, is given to few men to know. . . . In but two short weeks from this time I hope that you may enter, in your own homes, on a new series of readings, at which my assistance will be indispensable; but from these garish lights I vanish now for evermore, with a heartfelt, grateful, respectful, and affectionate farewell.[173]

A caricature of Dickens from 1870, the year of his death.

The Last Days of Charles Dickens

During April and May, Dickens continued to work on *Drood*. The first installment had "*very, very far outstripped every one of its predecessors,*" he reported, and he worked to make succeeding numbers as successful. "For the last week," he wrote during the fifth number, "I have been most perseveringly and ding-dong doggedly at work."[174]

Dickens had dinner with his trusted friend Forster on May 22, at what would prove to be their last meeting. During May, the author kept a full pace of social activities, and even entertained a young woman who hoped to be a writer. When she asked him what would happen if an author failed to complete a book before he died, Dickens replied, "Ah-h! That has occurred to me at times . . . [but] one can only work on, you know—work while it is day."[175]

The first week of June 1870 he attended the theater, always his greatest passion, and then returned to Gad's Hill. On June 8 he wrote all day, unusual for him since he never wrote more than a few hours at a time. But the next day he was going to London and wanted to deliver the text to the printer. Writing completed, he went into the house at 6:00 for dinner, looking very ill. When Georgina showed concern, however, he told her not to call for the doctor. Sitting at the table, his speech became slurred and he complained of a toothache. Suddenly he

Dickens: A Contradiction

Like most of his plots, Dickens's personality was complex. It was difficult to characterize him as a certain type of person. In Charles Dickens, *Brian Murray offers many insights into this contradictory man, including his love-hate relationship with money.*

"Even today, readers who know little or nothing about Dickens are likely to link him vaguely to children, animals, holiday dinners, and resilient good cheer. . . . [But] Dickens was not . . . Father Christmas. He was not instantly loved by all who crossed his path. . . .

Dickens hated hypocrisy as well as cruelty. He detested hypocrisy—a sin 'very prevalent in the Victorian era.'. . .

Dickens also detested the belief . . . that the pursuit of material gain was life's ultimate aim. One could fairly conclude that Dickens, or at least a large part of him, hated money itself. For money in Dickens's fiction is almost always associated with misery and ruin, with the warping of true feeling, and the thwarting of love."

put his hand to the side of his head, and asked for the window to be shut. Georgina went to him asking if he would like to lie down. "Yes," he replied, "on the ground," and he slipped down on his left side and lay unconscious, apparently stricken by an aneurysm in the brain.[176]

Doctors were summoned, but there was nothing they could do. Charles Dickens lived another twenty-four hours, breathing very heavily but never regaining consciousness. He died at 6:10 P.M. on Thursday, June 9, 1870, at the age of fifty-eight. In his will he had written that he wanted

> [to] be buried in an inexpensive, [simple], and strictly private manner; that no public announcement be made of the time or place of my burial; that at the ut-

most not more than three plain mourning coaches be employed; and that those who attend my funeral wear no scarf, cloak, black bow, long hat-band, or other such revolting absurdity.[177]

Dickens wished to be buried in the Rochester Cathedral graveyard, but Forster made arrangements to have his body interred at Westminster Abbey. The private service was, according to his wishes, simple. Although he had written many epitaphs for others, Dickens wanted only his name on his gravestone:

> I direct that my name be inscribed in plain English letters on my tomb. . . . I rest my claims to the remembrance of my country upon my published works, and to the remembrance of my friends upon their experience of me.[178]

9 A Great Celebrator of Life

> Few novelists have captured the wonder, caprice, and tragedy of life as well as Charles Dickens. . . . [He] continues to delight and teach—to enlighten all of humanity.
>
> —Brian Murray, *Charles Dickens*

He was a great spokesman against the social evils of his time, a great actor and performer, particularly of his own works. But Dickens's greatest gift was in portraying ordinary people common to most readers' lives. It was this ability to caricature common people in everyday situations that made him one of the greatest writers the world has known. His work involved the creation of nearly two thousand characters "born with Dickens but not dying with him, living on for ever." [179]

He rightly called himself "Inimitable." [180] He did not tell people how to live, he simply observed them living. This attitude made him a favorite among all classes in all generations. "Often," writes Brian Murray, "Dickens does seem more interested in observing than in reforming." In the Victorian Age of impeccable morals and prim-and-proper behavior, Dickens did not hold up "a blueprint for righteous living" [181] and insist that all people abide by it. Instead, notes critic John Carey, "Almost

any aberration, from drunkenness to wife-beating can be found eliciting at various times both Dickens's mournfulness and his amused toleration." [182]

For Dickens, life was a constant struggle between good and evil. This was the ultimate battle that each of his characters faced. Yet despite his fascination with violence, he never glorified it in his writing. In fact, he despised cruelty and fighting, and preferred instead to show the greatness of man's potential—to demonstrate that people are capable of fine, positive deeds.

Because this struggle is common to all generations, Dickens's writing has remained immortal. His characters have not become obsolete or unimportant to readers with the passing of time. The hopes, fears, and delights felt by Londoners of the mid-1800s are not unlike those of twenty-first-century people of all classes.

Dickens the Social Reformer

He criticized the squalid social conditions of nineteenth-century London. He hated the evil and injustice brought against common citizens by lawyers and government officials. And he was determined that his

Dickens sits for a photograph taken toward the end of his life. The process of photography was new and experimental through most of Dickens's lifetime.

writings would at least bring these conditions to light—at best, help to correct them.

The secret to Dickens's successful satire was his use of humor. "As a *comic* writer," observes Murray, "[he] shows unending delight in human diversity; he appears to accept quite serenely the inescapable fact that human beings are, in the final analysis, odd."[183]

Dickens knew the poor of London like no other writer, and because the poor are universal, he spoke for them worldwide. "London created Dickens," writes Peter Ackroyd, "just as Dickens created London. He came to it as a small, nervous child but

by the time of his death . . . he had recreated that city for the generations that followed."[184] Nor did Dickens ever forget that he was once one of London's poor. Even after his astounding successes, he continued to walk London's streets at night and converse with downtrodden locals.

As proof of his commitment to the poor, Dickens insisted that his novels be published in "numbers," or installments, at a price any reader could afford, for he believed that the poor had a right and a need to read as well as the rich and educated. "The English are, so far as I know, the hardest worked people on whom the sun shines," he once said. "Be content if in their wretched intervals of leisure they read for amusement and do no worse."[185]

The Dichotomy of Dickens

He was loved and beloved. He was championed by people of all countries and all social classes. For three days after his funeral, his grave remained open while thousands of admirers paid their last respects. Thousands more came in the days after his grave was closed. And yet, a year after his death, the *Times* of London wrote:

[He] was often vulgar in manners and dress, and often overbearing. . . . Ill at ease in his intercourse with gentlemen; that he preferred being a King in very low company; that even in his early days he lived rather in a clique than in society; that he was something of a Bohemian in his best moments—all these are truths.[186]

He was an impatient man. He loved his children, and yet in his later years he became increasingly frustrated by their lack of achievement and commitment to a goal. His daughter Kate, whom he had once considered his favorite child, told author

Mamie and Katey Dickens pose for a photo with their father at Gad's Hill in 1865.

Gladys Storey many years after his death, "my father was a wicked man—a very wicked man."[187]

Kate was referring, says Peter Ackroyd, to an illegitimate child that Dickens supposedly fathered with Ellen Ternan. The child was said to have died in infancy, but the truth of the rumor was never known. The image is a decided contradiction of Dickens the family man, but the author was decidedly a man of contradictions. Writes Ackroyd:

He was of genial [cheerful] disposition, but he also possessed an inflexible and paramount will. He often maintained a cool or grave demeanour, even while hiding the "savage" or "wild animal"

Charles Dickens's tomb at Westminster Abbey is testimony to the author's popularity and importance during his lifetime.

which he sometimes sensed within himself. . . . He worried a great deal, and yet maintained a determination to triumph over all difficulties. He had an unshakeable belief in his own rightness, and yet he was extraordinarily sensitive to criticism. . . . Many contemporaries saw these paradoxes, or disparities, and concluded that he was extremely "odd."[188]

The Importance of Charles Dickens

Dickens's incredibly accurate and detailed descriptions of life add a dimension to his work that is lacking in that of most other great novelists. "For what do Dickens's own novels tell us," asks Ackroyd, "but that a passing gesture, an image, or mood, can form a whole network of meaning. That the coincidence, the chance remark, the unexpected meeting, can change a human being."[189] These universal truths, with which nearly every person can identify, have made Charles Dickens one of the most beloved and most important authors of all time.

For half a century after his death, Dickens was all but ignored by critics. The stuffy, sentimental Victorian era had passed, and he appeared to pass with it.

New writers with more modern, avant-garde ideas were getting the attention. But a writer of Charles Dickens's caliber could not permanently fade from history. Wrote biographer Stephen Leacock in 1933:

> Transitory [temporary] popularity is not a proof of genius. But permanent popularity is. . . . Newer men come and go, rise and fall, and are forgotten. Dickens stays. Forty years ago newer writers were replacing Dickens; and thirty years ago; and twenty. The world today does not know their names. . . . In due time it will be known that the works of Charles Dickens represent the highest reach of the world's imaginative literature.[190]

Charles Dickens's popularity has become permanent, proof of his status as one of the world's great literary geniuses. His highest achievement is his ability to arouse universal emotions in readers of all generations and cultures. Writes Edgar Johnson:

> His passionate heart has long crumbled to dust. But the world he created shines with undying life, and the hearts of men still vibrate to his indignant anger, his love, his tears, his glorious laughter, and his triumphant faith in the dignity of man.[191]

Appendix A

Dickens's Major Works

(Dates indicate year of publication in book form. Most novels were
serialized prior to full-length publication.)

The Pickwick Papers, 1837

Oliver Twist, 1838

Nicholas Nickleby, 1839

The Old Curiosity Shop, 1841

Barnaby Rudge, 1841

A Christmas Carol, 1843

Martin Chuzzlewit, 1844

Dombey and Son, 1848

David Copperfield, 1850

Bleak House, 1853

Hard Times, 1854

Little Dorrit, 1857

A Tale of Two Cities, 1859

Great Expectations, 1861

Our Mutual Friend, 1865

The Mystery of Edwin Drood, 1870

Appendix B

Some of Dickens's Best-Known Characters

The Pickwick Papers:

Pickwick: the lovable, generous founder of the Pickwick Club

Sam Weller: sharp, shrewd young bootblack who is Pickwick's servant

Oliver Twist:

Oliver: the orphan who becomes "apprenticed" to a gang of thieves

Bumble: the tyrannical beadle in charge of Oliver's workhouse

Fagin: a Jew who is the chief trainer of new thieves in the gang

Bill Sikes: Fagin's brutal partner in the theft ring

Nancy: gang member who is in love with Sikes but kind to Oliver

Nicholas Nickleby:

Nicholas: young Englishman who becomes destitute when his father dies

Cheeryble brothers: upstanding, moral, benevolent employers of Nicholas

The Old Curiosity Shop:

Little Nell: an orphan, very devoted to the grandfather who is raising her

Quilp: a misshapen, cruel dwarf who is hunting Nell's grandfather for repayment of debts

Barnaby Rudge:

Barnaby: well-loved, feebleminded son of a convict who, with his talking raven Grip, foretells the nightmarish events tied to a murder on the day Barnaby was born

A Christmas Carol:

Ebenezer Scrooge: a miser whose life changes after a Christmas Eve vision

Jacob Marley: the ghost of Scrooge's former business partner

Tiny Tim: crippled son of Bob Cratchit, a clerk in Scrooge's countinghouse, who is famous for the line, "God bless us, every one"

Martin Chuzzlewit:

Seth Pecksniff: architect and land surveyor who considers himself a very moral and benevolent man, but who is the ultimate hypocrite

Sarah Gamp: a Cockney handywoman who likes to drink and becomes famous for her umbrella; one of Dickens's most humorous characters

Dombey and Son:

Dombey: a wealthy London merchant who puts all of his hopes and aspirations into his son, Paul, a sickly child who dies at an early age

Florence Dombey: sister to whom Paul is very devoted, but whom Dombey dislikes intensely

David Copperfield:

David: narrator said to be based on the character of Dickens himself

Clara Peggotty: kindly and devoted nurse and maid to young David's household

Wilkins Micawber: the always optimistic but improvident, unlucky father of a family with whom David lodges until Micawber is sent to debtors' prison; based on Dickens's father, John

Uriah Heep: hypocritical and villainous clerk in the office of Wickfield, the solicitor with whom David later lodges

Dora Spenlow: daughter of the lawyer with whom David studies, who later becomes his wife; character based on Maria Beadnell

Little Dorrit:

Amy Dorrit: child born in the Marshalsea debtors' prison; only one in her family to remain unchanged and good when her father comes into a fortune

Great Expectations:

Pip: an orphan who is grudgingly "brought up by hand" by his sister and her kindly blacksmith husband, Joe Gargery

Miss Havisham: an eccentric recluse who was deserted by her fiancé on her wedding day

Abel Magwitch: a convict who Pip helps to escape, and the provider of his "expectations"

Notes

Introduction: The Greatest English Novelist

1. Edgar Johnson, *Charles Dickens: His Tragedy and Triumph*. New York: Penguin Books, 1977, p. 7.

2. Brian Murray, *Charles Dickens*. New York: Continuum, 1994, p. 52.

3. Quoted in Murray, *Charles Dickens*, p. 16.

4. Quoted in Murray, *Charles Dickens*, p. 64.

5. Quoted in Murray, *Charles Dickens*, p. 20.

6. Quoted in *Encyclopaedia Britannica*, 15th ed., s.v. "Dickens, Charles."

7. Quoted in Piers Dudgeon, *Dickens' London*. London: Headline, 1989, p. 7.

Chapter 1: "The Secret Agony of My Soul"

8. Fred Kaplan, *Dickens: A Biography*. New York: William Morrow, 1988, p. 19.

9. Murray, *Charles Dickens*, p. 37.

10. Kaplan, *Dickens*, p. 21.

11. Norman and Jeanne MacKenzie, *Dickens: A Life*. New York: Oxford University Press, 1979, p. 7.

12. Quoted in MacKenzie, *Dickens*, p. 7.

13. Quoted in Johnson, *Charles Dickens*, p. 18.

14. Quoted in Dudgeon, *Dickens' London*, p. 51.

15. Quoted in Murray, *Charles Dickens*, p. 37.

16. Quoted in Kaplan, *Dickens*, p. 38.

17. Quoted in Dudgeon, *Dickens' London*, p. 7.

18. Quoted in Dudgeon, *Dickens' London*, p. 115.

19. Quoted in Peter Ackroyd, *Dickens*. New York: HarperCollins, 1990, p. 95.

20. Quoted in Murray, *Charles Dickens*, p. 40.

21. Quoted in Murray, *Charles Dickens*, p. 40.

22. Quoted in Dudgeon, *Dickens' London*, pp. 7–8.

Chapter 2: "My Eyes Were So Dimmed with Joy and Pride"

23. Kaplan, *Dickens*, pp. 47–48.

24. Quoted in Kaplan, *Dickens*, p. 49.

25. Quoted in Johnson, *Charles Dickens*, pp. 50–51.

26. Quoted in MacKenzie, *Dickens*, p. 26.

27. Quoted in MacKenzie, *Dickens*, p. 26.

28. Johnson, *Charles Dickens*, p. 345.

29. Edward Guiliano and Philip Collins, eds., *The Annotated Dickens*, vol. 2. New York: Clarkson N. Potter, 1986, p. 267.

30. Quoted in Murray, *Charles Dickens*, p. 42.

31. Johnson, *Charles Dickens*, p. 51.

32. Quoted in MacKenzie, *Dickens*, p. 21.

33. Quoted in Ackroyd, *Dickens*, p. 473.

34. Quoted in Murray, *Charles Dickens*, p. 41.

35. Quoted in Murray, *Charles Dickens*, p. 41.

36. Ackroyd, *Dickens*, p. 140.

37. Angus Wilson, *The World of Charles Dickens*. New York: Viking Press, 1970, p. 94.

38. Stephen Leacock, *Charles Dickens: His Life and Work*. Garden City, NY: Doubleday Doran, 1933, p. 22.

39. Quoted in Leacock, *Charles Dickens*, p. 22.

40. Quoted in Johnson, *Charles Dickens*, p. 73.

41. Quoted in MacKenzie, *Dickens*, p. 29.

42. Quoted in MacKenzie, *Dickens*, p. 31.

43. Quoted in Murray, *Charles Dickens*, p. 18.

44. Johnson, *Charles Dickens*, p. 78.

45. Quoted in MacKenzie, *Dickens*, p. 32.

46. MacKenzie, *Dickens*, p. 32.

47. Quoted in MacKenzie, *Dickens*, p. 32.

Chapter 3: A Sudden and Astounding Rise to Eminence

48. MacKenzie, *Dickens*, pp. 40–41.

49. Quoted in Frank N. Magill, ed., *Masterplots*. Englewood Cliffs, NJ: Salem Press, 1949, p. 3,652.

50. Wilson, *The World of Charles Dickens*, pp. 115–16.

51. Ackroyd, *Dickens*, p. 182.

52. Murray, *Charles Dickens*, dust jacket.

53. Leacock, *Charles Dickens*, p. 28.

54. Magill, *Masterplots*, p. 3,652.

55. Quoted in Ackroyd, *Dickens*, p. 161.

56. Quoted in Ackroyd, *Dickens*, p. 187.

57. Quoted in Murray, *Charles Dickens*, p. 46.

58. Quoted in MacKenzie, *Dickens*, pp. 57–58.

59. Quoted in Johnson, *Charles Dickens*, pp. 125–26.

60. Quoted in MacKenzie, *Dickens*, p. 55.

61. Quoted in Dudgeon, *Dickens' London*, p. 17.

62. Guiliano and Collins, *The Annotated Dickens*, vol. 1, p. 800.

63. Dudgeon, *Dickens' London*, p. 139.

64. Quoted in *Encyclopaedia Britannica*, 15th ed., s.v. "Dickens, Charles."

65. Quoted in Johnson, *Charles Dickens*, p. 137.

66. Ackroyd, *Dickens*, pp. 249–50.

67. Ackroyd, *Dickens*, p. 251.

68. Magill, *Masterplots*, p. 3,267.

69. Charles Dickens, *Nicholas Nickleby*. Chicago: M. A. Donohue, n.d., p. 157.

70. Quoted in Magill, *Masterplots*, p. 3,358.

71. Quoted in Johnson, *Charles Dickens*, p. 138.

72. Quoted in Kaplan, *Dickens*, p. 86.

73. Murray, *Charles Dickens*, p. 51.

74. Quoted in Murray, *Charles Dickens*, p. 15.

75. Quoted in Kaplan, *Dickens*, p. 129.

76. Quoted in Frank Donovan, *Dickens and Youth*. New York: Dodd, Mead, 1968, pp. 102–103.

77. Kaplan, *Dickens*, pp. 120–21.

Chapter 4: "Unbounded Praise, Unstinted Hospitality"

78. Quoted in Johnson, *Charles Dickens*, p. 194.

79. Quoted in MacKenzie, *Dickens*, p. 110.

80. Quoted in Leacock, *Charles Dickens*, p. 68.

81. Quoted in Johnson, *Charles Dickens*, p. 207.

82. Quoted in Leacock, *Charles Dickens*, p. 74.

83. Leacock, *Charles Dickens*, p. 75.

84. Quoted in MacKenzie, *Dickens*, p. 119.

85. Quoted in MacKenzie, *Dickens*, p. 118.

86. Quoted in Murray, *Charles Dickens*, p. 50.

87. Quoted in Johnson, *Charles Dickens*, p. 210.

88. Quoted in MacKenzie, *Dickens*, p. 119.

89. Quoted in Murray, *Charles Dickens*, p. 49.

90. Quoted in Johnson, *Charles Dickens*, p. 218.

91. Quoted in MacKenzie, *Dickens*, p. 120.

92. Quoted in Johnson, *Charles Dickens*, p. 222.

93. Quoted in Johnson, *Charles Dickens*, p. 220.

94. Quoted in Kaplan, *Dickens*, p. 137.

95. Quoted in Kaplan, *Dickens*, p. 137.

96. Quoted in MacKenzie, *Dickens*, p. 123.

97. Quoted in MacKenzie, *Dickens*, p. 124.

98. Quoted in Murray, *Charles Dickens*, p. 49.

99. Quoted in Wilson, *The World of Charles Dickens*, p. 170.

100. Quoted in Johnson, *Charles Dickens*, p. 233.

101. Leacock, *Charles Dickens*, p. 96.

102. Quoted in Johnson, *Charles Dickens*, p. 235.

103. Quoted in MacKenzie, *Dickens*, p. 126.

104. Quoted in Leacock, *Charles Dickens*, pp. 101–102.

105. Leacock, *Charles Dickens*, p. 100.

Chapter 5: The Highest Reach of His Achievement

106. Quoted in Ackroyd, *Dickens*, p. 33.

107. Ackroyd, *Dickens*, p. 33.

108. Donovan, *Dickens and Youth*, p. 217.

109. Donovan, *Dickens and Youth*, pp. 223–24.

110. Quoted in Johnson, *Charles Dickens*, p. 260.

111. Quoted in Leacock, *Charles Dickens*, p. 116.

112. Leacock, *Charles Dickens*, p. 125.

113. Kaplan, *Dickens*, p. 197.

114. Quoted in Murray, *Charles Dickens*, p. 57.

115. Quoted in Murray, *Charles Dickens*, p. 112.

116. Quoted in Murray, *Charles Dickens*, p. 55.

117. Quoted in MacKenzie, *Dickens*, p. 213.

118. Quoted in MacKenzie, *Dickens*, p. 214.

119. Quoted in Johnson, *Charles Dickens*, p. 355.

120. Leacock, *Charles Dickens*, p. 144.

121. Leacock, *Charles Dickens*, p. 146.

122. Quoted in Leacock, *Charles Dickens*, p. 142.

123. Quoted in Ackroyd, *Dickens*, p. 620.

124. Quoted in Johnson, *Charles Dickens*, p. 377.

125. Quoted in Murray, *Charles Dickens*, p. 59.

126. Charles Dickens, *A Child's History of England*. Chicago: M. A. Donohue, n.d., pp. 140–41.

127. Leacock, *Charles Dickens*, p. 166.

Chapter 6: Bobbing Up Corkwise from a Sea of Hard Times

128. Johnson, *Charles Dickens*, pp. 254–55.

129. Quoted in MacKenzie, *Dickens*, p. 246.

130. Leacock, *Charles Dickens*, p. 159.

131. MacKenzie, *Dickens*, p. 256.

132. Quoted in Johnson, *Charles Dickens*, p. 406.

133. Guiliano and Collins, *The Annotated Dickens*, vol. 1, p. 893.

134. Quoted in *Encyclopaedia Britannica*, 15th ed., s.v. "Dickens, Charles" p. 709.

135. Quoted in Johnson, *Charles Dickens*, p. 417.

136. Quoted in Johnson, *Charles Dickens*, p. 442.

137. Quoted in Johnson, *Charles Dickens*, p. 442.

138. Johnson, *Charles Dickens*, p. 434.

139. Quoted in Johnson, *Charles Dickens*, p. 448.

140. Quoted in MacKenzie, *Dickens*, pp. 298–99.

141. MacKenzie, *Dickens*, p. 291.

142. Quoted in Murray, *Charles Dickens*, p. 65.

Chapter 7: "It Was the Best of Times, It Was the Worst of Times"

143. Leacock, *Charles Dickens*, pp. 224–25.

144. Ackroyd, *Dickens*, p. 885.

145. Quoted in Johnson, *Charles Dickens*, p. 485.

146. Quoted in Kaplan, *Dickens*, p. 439.

147. Ackroyd, *Dickens*, p. 938.

148. Quoted in Leacock, *Charles Dickens*, p. 237.

149. Murray, *Charles Dickens*, p. 66.

150. Johnson, *Charles Dickens*, p. 487.

151. Murray, *Charles Dickens*, p. 69.

152. Leacock, *Charles Dickens*, p. 239.

153. Quoted in Leacock, *Charles Dickens*, p. 239.

154. Murray, *Charles Dickens*, p. 69.

155. Quoted in Murray, *Charles Dickens*, p. 69.

156. Quoted in Murray, *Charles Dickens*, p. 16.

157. Leacock, *Charles Dickens*, p. 31.

Chapter 8: "I Vanish Now for Evermore"

158. Quoted in Ackroyd, *Dickens*, p. 963.

159. Murray, *Charles Dickens*, p. 69.

160. Johnson, *Charles Dickens*, pp. 532–33.

161. Quoted in Johnson, *Charles Dickens*, p. 539.

162. Johnson, *Charles Dickens*, p. 540.

163. Quoted in Johnson, *Charles Dickens*, p. 547.

164. Leacock, *Charles Dickens*, p. 268.

165. Johnson, *Charles Dickens*, p. 553.

166. Quoted in Kaplan, *Dickens*, p. 539.

167. Ackroyd, *Dickens*, p. 19.

168. Wilson, *The World of Charles Dickens*, pp. 290–91.

169. Kaplan, *Dickens*, p. 548.

170. Quoted in Ackroyd, *Dickens*, p. 1,065.

171. Kaplan, *Dickens*, p. 550.

172. Ackroyd, *Dickens*, p. 1,066.

173. Quoted in Kaplan, *Dickens*, pp. 548–49.

174. Quoted in Johnson, *Charles Dickens*, p. 576.

175. Quoted in Johnson, *Charles Dickens*, p. 577.

176. MacKenzie, *Dickens*, p. 390.

177. Quoted in Murray, *Charles Dickens*, p. 71.

178. Quoted in MacKenzie, *Dickens*, p. 391.

Chapter 9: A Great Celebrator of Life

179. Ackroyd, *Dickens*, p. 2.

180. Wilson, *The World of Charles Dickens*, p. 297.

181. Murray, *Charles Dickens*, pp. 22–23.

182. Quoted in Murray, *Charles Dickens*, p. 23.

183. Murray, *Charles Dickens*, p. 23.

184. Quoted in Dudgeon, *Dickens' London*, p. 7.

185. Quoted in Murray, *Charles Dickens*, opening epigraph.

186. Quoted in Murray, *Charles Dickens*, p. 71.

187. Quoted in Murray, *Charles Dickens*, p. 34.

188. Ackroyd, *Dickens*, p. 950.

189. Ackroyd, *Dickens*, p. 1,082.

190. Leacock, *Charles Dickens*, p. 307.

191. Johnson, *Charles Dickens*, p. 583.

For Further Reading

Jane Louise Curry, *What the Dickens!* New York: McElderry Books, 1991. Fiction set in 1842 when Dickens is touring America. Eleven-year-old twins learn of a plan to steal the author's newly finished novel.

Charles Haines, *Charles Dickens.* New York: Franklin Watts, 1969. A biography in the Immortals of Literature series, 180 pages.

Spencer Johnson, *The Value of Imagination: The Story of Charles Dickens.* La Jolla, CA: Value Communications, 1977. A book for readers ages six through twelve that uses the life of Charles Dickens to emphasize the value of an imaginative mind.

Elisabeth Kyle, *Great Ambitions: A Story of the Early Years of Charles Dickens.* New York: Holt, Rinehart & Winston, 1968. Biography of Dickens from the age of twelve through his early married life.

Diane Stanley and Peter Vennema, *Charles Dickens: The Man Who Had Great Expectations.* New York: Morrow Junior Books, 1993. Follows the life and writing career of the novelist and includes color illustrations.

Katharine Elliott Wilkie, *Charles Dickens: The Inimitable Boz.* New York: Abelard-Schuman, 1970. Biography of the novelist in 188 pages, with illustrations.

Works Consulted

Peter Ackroyd, *Dickens*. New York: Harper-Collins, 1990. A twelve-hundred-page account of Dickens's life; its author has been called his most exhaustive and exhausting biographer.

Frank Donovan, *Dickens and Youth*. New York: Dodd, Mead, 1968. Describes the world of Dickens through his child characters: who they were, what they did, how he conceived and handled them.

Piers Dudgeon, *Dickens' London*. London: Headline, 1989. Photo history of London in Dickens's time, with extensive quotations from his books.

Edward Guiliano and Philip Collins, eds., *The Annotated Dickens*. Vols. 1 and 2. New York: Clarkson N. Potter, 1986. Includes text, illustrations, annotations, and introductions to *David Copperfield, A Tale of Two Cities, Great Expectations, The Pickwick Papers, Oliver Twist, A Christmas Carol,* and *Hard Times*.

Edgar Johnson, *Charles Dickens: His Tragedy and Triumph*. New York: Penguin Books, 1977. Considered the finest of the literary biographies of Dickens.

Fred Kaplan, *Dickens: A Biography*. New York: William Morrow, 1988. A six-hundred-plus-page full-scale portrait of Dickens by a noted biographer and literary scholar.

Stephen Leacock, *Charles Dickens: His Life and Work*. Garden City, NY: Doubleday Doran, 1933. A biography and analysis of Dickens's work sixty years after the author's death.

Norman and Jeanne MacKenzie, *Dickens: A Life*. New York: Oxford University Press, 1979. Shows "the whole" Dickens: novelist, family man, and friend to the literati and common people alike.

Frank N. Magill, ed., *Masterplots*. Englewood Cliffs, NJ: Salem Press, 1949. A multivolume set that offers short critiques and synopses of major literary works, including all the Dickens novels.

Brian Murray, *Charles Dickens*. New York: Continuum, 1994. A short (two-hundred-page) but insightful overview of Dickens's life and writings.

Angus Wilson, *The World of Charles Dickens*. New York: Viking Press, 1970. A beautifully illustrated biography that paints a fine picture of Victorian England and quotes extensively from Dickens's books to capture the essence of his life.

Index

lost childhood theme in, 32
principal characters in, 82
public readings from, 62
social criticisms in, 52
Our Mutual Friend, 65

"Phiz." *See* Browne, Hablot Knight
Pickwick Club, 27
Pickwick Papers, The, 27–29, 32, 62
Pictures from Italy, 45
politics, 24
Portsmouth, England, 12
Posthumous Papers of the Pickwick Club. See Pickwick Papers, The
public readings, by Dickens
in America, 68–69
fulfilled desire to act, 62
in London, 70, 72–73
satisfied need for attention, 57

Ragged Schools, 52

schools
boarding, 33, 34

conditions in, 33–34, 52, 55
self-sacrifice, 62
Seymour, Robert, 26, 27
Shaw, George Bernard, 66
shorthand, 19
Sketches by Boz, 26, 27, 32
slavery, 41
social criticisms, (Dickens's)
of debtors' prisons, 57
of educational system, 33–34, 52, 55
of Industrial Revolution, 48, 52, 55, 57, 75–76
of poverty in London, 10, 32, 35–36
of Victorian social values, 44, 57, 62, 65, 74
Strange Gentleman, The, 30
Sumner, Charles, 38

Tale of Two Cities, A, 60–62
Ternan, Ellen, 59, 78
Thackeray, William Makepeace, 48
Thames River, 50
Thoreau, Henry David, 48
train tragedy, 67
travels, by Dickens

to Boston, 37–38, 68–69
to Boulogne, France, 53
to Canada, 42
to the Continent, 44–45
to New York, 38–40, 69
in Switzerland and Paris, 47
train accident, 67
True Sun (newspaper), 22
Tyler, John, 41

Uncle John, 58
Uncommercial Traveller, The, 50, 64

Victoria (queen of England), 70, 72
Victorian society, 44, 57, 62, 65, 74
Village Coquettes, The, 30

Warren's Blacking Factory, 15–17
Weller, Mary, 14
Wellington House Academy, 17–18
Wills, William H., 51, 64
Wits Miscellany, 30
women, 18

Picture Credits

Cover photo: National Archives

The Bettmann Archive, 34

Corbis-Bettmann, 10, 24, 28, 45, 46, 48, 50, 53, 54, 57, 60, 61, 63, 64

Dickens House, 15, 16, 18, 20, 21, 23, 30 (both), 39, 43

Library of Congress, 22, 33, 66, 72, 76

Joseph Paris Picture Archive, 25, 77

Picture Collection, The Branch Libraries, The New York Public Library, 12, 13, 36, 73

About the Author

Eleanor H. Ayer is author of more than fifty books, most for children and young adults. Among them are several biographies, including *Adolf Hitler* in The Importance Of series. She has written a variety of books on social issues such as *Teen Marriage, Depression,* and *Homeless Children,* as well as several books on the Holocaust and World War II.

Mrs. Ayer has a master's degree in literacy journalism from Syracuse University's Newhouse School of Journalism. The mother of two boys, she lives in Frederick, Colorado, where she and her husband operate a small book-publishing company.